PRAISE FOR BOB COSTAS AND FAIR BALL

"[*Fair Ball* is] the pick of the litter when it comes to this season's baseball books. Costas is witty, sharp-tongued, and clear headed, a rare-triple play combination. . . . Reading Bob Costas is like getting a seat at a ballpark next to someone who loves the game but has been spared the blindness that afflicts so many lovers. The book is a joy to read."   —Stephen King

"Bob Costas is as witty, insightful and entertaining behind a word processor as he is behind a microphone."
                                          —*Pittsburgh Post-Gazette*

"Bob Costas just hit one out of the park."
                                          —*New Orleans Times-Picayune*

"Costas is that rare hybrid in sportscasting with converging wit, erudition and superb communication skills."
                                          —*Los Angeles Times*

"Damned by fools as a baseball purist . . . Costas's right-headed activism and devotion to the game as a broadcaster, journalist and fan have been deep, unwavering and gutsy."
                                          —*TV Guide*

"[Costas] understands the special niche baseball once enjoyed and wants to see it restored . . . *Fair Ball* offers a thoughtful blueprint for accomplishing that."
                                          —*Cleveland Plain Dealer*

"[Costas] is the best sportscaster of his generation because he's funny and well-spoken and a brilliant interviewer."
—*Kansas City Star*

"*Fair Ball* is concise, orderly, witty and, above all, logical."
—*Boston Globe*

"With his unique ability to weave intellect into a typically anti-intellectual medium, he's the best in the business."
—*P.O.V.*

"*Fair Ball* is carefully thought out, logically developed and . . . passionately argued.   —*Booklist*

"Intelligent, witty, good-natured, Costas is the very antithesis of the shills who dominate most sports programming."
—*People*

"He is knowledgeable, engaging, even-handed and appropriately sarcastic."   —*Orlando Sentinel*

"He is as good a pure broadcaster as I've ever seen."
—Charlie Rose

FAIR BALL

A Fan's Case for Baseball

BOB COSTAS

BROADWAY BOOKS
New York

BROADWAY

A hardcover edition of this book was published in 2000
by Broadway Books.

FAIR BALL. Copyright © 2000 by Robert Costas. Foreword
Copyright © 2001 by Andrew Zimbalist. All rights reserved. Printed in
the United States of America. No part of this book may be reproduced
or transmitted in any form or by any means, electronic or mechanical,
including photocopying, recording, or by any information storage
and retrieval system, without written permission from the publisher.
For information, address Broadway Books, a division of
Random House, Inc., 1540 Broadway, New York, NY 10036.

Broadway Books titles may be purchased for business or
promotional use or for special sales. For information, please write to:
Special Markets Department, Random House, Inc.,
1540 Broadway, New York, NY 10036.

BROADWAY BOOKS and its logo, a letter B bisected on the diagonal, are
trademarks of Broadway Books, a division of Random House, Inc.

Designed by Tina Thompson

The Library of Congress has established a
cataloging-in-publication record for this title.

ISBN-10: 0-7679-0466-4

ISBN-13: 978-0-7679-0466-7

For John Costas,
who saw the dice go cold too often

CONTENTS

A Note to the Reader

Fair Ball was published in hardcover in April 2000. As the paperback comes out a year later, the editors at Broadway Books asked me to write an afterword, commenting on the developments of the past year. I in turn asked Dr. Andrew Zimbalist, of Smith College, to add his perspective in the form of a foreword. Dr. Zimbalist is one of America's most respected authorities on the economics of sports. His books, articles, and commentaries have been an important part of the baseball debate for many years. I'm grateful for his contribution here.

B.C.

FOREWORD

by Andrew Zimbalist

Baseball, once again, is at a crossroads. The current collective-bargaining agreement ends after the 2001 season. Each time an agreement has expired since 1972 there has been a work stoppage, and the players and owners appear to be on yet another collision course.

Equally foreboding, competition on the playing field has become acutely imbalanced. Since 1995 only three out of 189 postseason games have been won by teams in the bottom half of payrolls. That is, these teams have less than 1 chance in 50 of qualifying for and then winning a postseason game—worse than the odds that a voter pushed a chad for Ralph Nader in November 2000!

Accompanying this inequality between rich and poor teams has been dominance by the New York Yankees, with their stadium revenues in excess of $95 million and their local media contracts of nearly $60 million annually. This Yankee hegemony has led some analysts to proclaim: What's the big deal—just another Yankee dynasty.

The Pollyannaish commentators, in part, are being deceived by some superficial indicators of success. Baseball's problems in its low- and middle-revenue markets have been partially obscured by the durability feats of Cal Ripken and the slugging heroics of Mark McGwire and Sammy Sosa, as well as the opening of a dozen new ball-parks and a protracted economic boom in the country since the early 1990s. True, the game's total revenues have continued to grow and its total attendance has set new records. These records, however, were largely a product of adding four expansion teams during the past decade; average attendance per game by 2000 still had not recovered to its 1994 levels—and this despite the fact that more than one-third of the teams were playing in new facilities. Meanwhile, regular and postseason network television ratings have continued to plummet.

And, in part, the glossy-eyed analysts are overlooking the obvious. First, the good old days of the last Yankee dynasty, 1949–64, were not that good for baseball after all. In that span, average attendance at games grew by less than 3 percent over the entire fifteen years, even though real ticket prices remained virtually flat (they increased by less than half of one percent per year). Yet during the same period, real disposable incomes in the United States grew by 74 percent. Moreover, four and five decades ago baseball stood alone on the pedestal of popular team sports. Today, it has been surpassed by the NFL and is seriously challenged by the NBA as well as by the growing list of new professional sports and entertainment options on television and the Internet.

Second, there is clear evidence today that the problem is not just the Yankees, but it is the growing disparity between the top- and bottom-revenue teams. Just eleven years ago, in 1989, the revenue difference between the highest and lowest teams was around $30 million. In 1999, this difference grew more than fivefold to over $160 million. And the correlation between team win percentage and team payroll has been significant at the highest statistical level every year between 1995 and 2000—and not significant at this level in any year between 1985 and 1994.

Moreover, increasingly it is not only the difference in revenues among individual teams but the synergies between a team and the owner's other businesses that drive payroll inequality. Rupert Murdoch hopes that Kevin Brown will promote his international media interests; Tom Hicks expects Rodriguez to lift the value of the 250-odd acres he is developing around the ballpark at Arlington along with raising the value of the stadium's naming rights; and Steinbrenner looks for Mussina to cement the formation of a new sportschannel in the Big Apple.

In *Fair Ball*, Bob Costas clearly and cogently documents how baseball crossed over the line of acceptable imbalance in the mid-1990s. In the Afterword to this paperback edition, Costas compellingly responds to those who claim that all returned to normal in 2000. After all, they ask, didn't the low-payroll Oakland A's, San Francisco Giants, and Chicago White Sox make it into the playoffs, and didn't the spread between the top performing team (.599) and the bottom performing team (.401) narrow to under 200 points?

Sure, but the A's, Giants, and White Sox collectively won only three games in the entire postseason and the spread in win percentages has little to do with the competitive balance that fans care about. Baseball owners try to assemble enough good players to win a championship, not enough good players to reach a maximum win percentage.

Baseball's real concern is not whether the range of win percentages is 200 or 240 points in any particular year, but whether the same teams are always on top and whether these are the teams with the highest revenues. It is the latter factor that will determine the fan's sense of how level the playing field is.

In all professional team sports, winning goes in cycles. No team, not even the Yankees, always wins. As players age, a team's competitiveness wanes. New players must be acquired and new team chemistries must be fashioned. It is natural that some turnover at the top will occur. It is also natural that an occasional team with a lower payroll will rise due to effective management, strong farm systems, and good luck. The issue is not whether there are exceptions, such as Oakland in 2000, but whether or not there are patterns. Ask the fans in Milwaukee, Montreal, and Minnesota if there are patterns.

In fact, baseball's hierarchy perceived the game's growing imbalance problems back in 1996 when the last collective-bargaining agreement was finally signed. Part of this agreement attempted to alleviate this problem by introducing a new revenue-sharing system and a luxury tax on the teams with the five highest payrolls in the two leagues. Ironically, by being "too little, too late" and providing perverse incentives, as Costas explains in these pages, this new plan actually exacerbated the inequality. Last year, the bottom three clubs in revenue (the Expos, the Twins, and the Marlins) received $24 million, $22 million, and $16 million respectively in transfers from the 1996-designed revenue sharing system.

Given that at least the bottom half of teams recognize that they have no hope to compete in the free agent market, their best profit-maximizing strategy is to lowball their payroll, perform poorly and collect large transfers from the rich teams. Little wonder, then, that the bottom half of teams got worse, as the top teams pulled in millions of additional dollars from the local media deals and new stadiums.

Diagnosing the illness, of course, is just the first step. The next step, identifying and implementing a remedy, is more difficult. It not only requires the players and the owners to find common ground; it necessitates that the owners reach an accord among themselves. As Costas points out, historically the latter has been as unlikely as the former. The owners disparate economic circumstances make it improbable that they will produce a coherent vision about what needs to be done. As the recent dissension following the megacontract of Alex

Rodriguez lays bare, it is much easier for the owners to snipe at each other than to plan productively for the game's future.

The tragedy is that when the owners can't agree on a sensible plan for reform, they tend to fall back on the only strategy that pleases them all: bash the players. Whether or not some restriction in player markets ought to be part of the solution, when it is presented absent a cohesive plan for change, the Players Association naturally bridles at the perception that the entire burden of rectifying the game's errant course is being placed on their backs. The prerequisite for righting baseball and avoiding yet another work stoppage is that the owners put their individual, short-term interests aside long enough to get their act together. This will require strong leadership. At the end of the day, whether or not this leadership is provided will be the acid test of the Selig commissionership.

So, what is the best plan for baseball? Bud Selig commissioned a Blue Ribbon Panel of four pundits—Paul Volcker, George Mitchell, Richard Levin, and George Will—to come up with a plan. With abundant resources and staff to study the game and a year and a half to contemplate a remedy, the Panel came out with a series of recommendations in July 2000. Interestingly, their plan closely resembles that proposed by Costas, working alone, in *Fair Ball*, originally published in April 2000. Indeed, the approaches are so similar that it would not have been inaccurate for the next day's headlines to read:

"Blue Ribbon Panel Endorses the Costas plan." (To be sure, there are differences, and Costas comments on these in his Afterword.)

Briefly, each plan calls for enhanced revenue sharing, additional player market restrictions, and alterations in baseball's draft system. Significantly, each plan calls for an initial minimum team payroll of $40 million to derail owners attempting to free ride on redistributive transfers. I do not agree with all the reform elements proposed by Costas or the Panel, but their proposals are sensible and offer an excellent starting point for the upcoming negotiations.

Before presenting his reform suggestions in *Fair Ball*, Costas issues this caveat (p. 14): "I do not presume to have all the answers. But I hope that in many cases I'm on the right track. And at the very least, these things are worth discussing. That discussion should help us arrive at better answers than the ones we've been getting lately."

Costas then proceeds to challenge the prevailing wisdom of both the owners and players. One can only hope that Costas' commitment to taking a fresh and probing look at the game and his willingness to be open-minded and flexible about the best path to baseball's economic reform will be mimicked in the coming months by the owners and the players as they sit down to hammer out a new collective bargaining agreement.

Of course, Costas ranges well beyond the strictly economic aspects of baseball reform. From realignment to the playoff structure, from the designated hitter to interleague play, Costas offers passionate and provocative ideas that Major League Baseball would do well to consider seriously.

Whatever baseball's powers choose to do, however, in the pages that follow the reader should prepare for an engaging and insightful discussion of what ails our national pastime and what can be done to improve it.

Andrew Zimbalist is a noted authority on the economics of sports and the author of *Baseball and Billions: A Probing Look Inside the Big Business of Our National Pastime*. He is currently the Robert A. Woods professor of economics at Smith College.

FAIR BALL

INTRODUCTION

Let's say it's late October, and you're in what should be baseball heaven, sitting on the couch watching the fourth game of the World Series, Yanks vs. Braves.

Suppose for a moment that you're a Minnesota Twins fan. You've been a baseball fan all your life, grew up playing the game, once got Rod Carew's autograph at a Little League clinic, spent your eighth birthday at Metropolitan Stadium in Bloomington, and your fifteenth at the Humpdome in downtown Minneapolis. You played baseball in high school, took a summer vacation in college to Cooperstown, and once joked that you wouldn't leave the country between September 1 and the end of October, because you couldn't stand to miss the end of a pennant race or the playoffs.

But tonight you find yourself watching the Series not because you're passionately rooting for either the Atlanta Braves or the New York Yankees. Instead you're watching mostly because, well, watching the Series is what you've done every October for as long as you can remember (save for that lost fall of 1994).

So you sit there and contemplate the Atlanta Braves,

a team the Twins vanquished eight years earlier in perhaps the greatest Series ever. And you wonder about the fortunes and forces that, since then, have sent your club into a decade-long financial and competitive tailspin, while the Braves have been in the playoffs every full season since. The two cities are roughly the same size, and, competitive factors being equal, Minnesota has supported the Twins at least as well as Atlanta has supported its team. Yet in the weird logic of late-'90s baseball, Atlanta is a big market and Minneapolis–St. Paul is a small one. While your team still plays in the depressing dome, Atlanta has a new state-of-the-art facility with natural grass, good sight lines, a cozy retro feel, and all the modern amenities.

When you look across the field at the New York Yankees, you just shake your head. It's hard to work up the old "Damn Yankees" antipathy these days. Partly because of Joe Torre, and partly because baseball's proudest franchise seems to be playing in a league, if not a sport, entirely different from your own. They got your best player two years ago, even though the Twins' owners would have paid him a team-record contract to stay in Minnesota. He wanted to go to another club, Chuck Knoblauch said, because he wanted to play for a title. You recall that as a rookie Knoblauch had won a World Series ring. He was a Twin, and it was your team's second world championship in five seasons. You were sure then that Knoblauch would be a Minnesota fixture.

But these days, you know better. No player of consistent All-Star quality is going to remain in Minnesota throughout his career. And yet just this summer, you watched George Brett—who played as recently as 1993—inducted into the Hall of Fame. Brett played his whole career with Kansas City, passing up bigger offers elsewhere. Not that he wasn't well-compensated, both financially and competitively. His Royals were perennial contenders, and won the AL West six times. He was happy to stay. Yet if he came up today, his competitive nature would make a move not just probable, but mandatory—not because of greed or disloyalty, but because teams like Kansas City and Minnesota can no longer even hope to compete.

Now back to the Yankees. After winning their second Series in three years, with a payroll that was already four times that of the Twins, they began the 1999 season by trading for the Cy Young Award winner, Roger Clemens. He's a pitcher you've long respected, but one who has bewildered you in recent years: Hadn't the Texan Clemens said he wanted to be closer to home after leaving the Boston Red Sox in '97? So didn't his decision to sign with the Toronto Blue Jays betray either a disingenuous streak or a staggeringly bad grasp of geography? But Clemens can pitch, so he proceeded to win two straight Cy Young Awards for the Blue Jays. Then Clemens demanded a trade in '99, because, he said, he wanted to play with a contender. And you wondered, "If a team like Toronto—

which won back-to-back World Series in '92 and '93, and only recently drew 4 million fans for a season to a new ballpark—can't qualify as a contender, what does that tell you?" And all through the '99 season, as the pitching-shy Blue Jays were fighting toward the brink of contention on the bats of talented young sluggers like Carlos Delgado and Shawn Green, you couldn't help wondering how good they might be if they still had Clemens pitching for them.

After Clemens closes out the Series in Game 4, with a vintage, overpowering performance, you wonder if all this means the same thing to him as it would have if he'd stayed with the Red Sox and they'd somehow won it all. Or if it means anything like what it meant to Kirby Puckett, who took less money to stay in Minnesota, where he won world championships in 1987 and 1991.

In the weeks ahead, instead of the normal shake-up of hot-stove action, the rich get richer, and the ranks of those who can no longer compete grows to include what once were considered "middle-market" clubs. Seattle has a brand-new stadium and a string of sellouts, but they're convinced they'll have to trade Ken Griffey Jr. and/or Alex Rodriguez. Toronto is working on deals to ship away Green and Delgado before they bolt for free agency.

You still call yourself a baseball fan, and you still get out to the Metrodome a few times a season. But the game seems more distant today than it did only a few years ago. You can't follow pennant races anymore—because there aren't any—and the wild card seems hard to get excited about. The media characterizes the game as "on the way back," thanks largely to Mark McGwire and Sammy Sosa. But even at its most epic, the '98 home-run race seemed somewhat disconnected from the season it was part of—less a highlight of the season itself than a thing unto itself (through no fault of the particulars), or a substitute for the plain fact that when the last several baseball seasons began, you knew that your team had no living chance to contend for a pennant.

No, the rising tide has not lifted all boats. And as you watch the games from your living room now, you realize that something essential has changed. You're not nostalgic for the "old days" as much as you are for the more recent ones, when the fact that you had one of the best managers and farm systems in baseball was a crucial advantage. When star players wanted to be with the Twins. When the Twins' owners weren't eyeing other cities. And when you could greet April with the belief that your team had a prayer.

But as you sit and watch the Yankees celebrate, those days seem far removed. You might wonder if anyone on the other side of the screen is feeling the same way.

Let's go back a couple years, and let me tell you about the experience of another fan on another night. . . .

The third game of the 1997 World Series was already three-and-a-half-hours old, the scoreboard clock in Cleveland was approaching midnight, and the thermometer was dropping toward freezing.

But as the Cleveland Indians took the field for the top half of the ninth inning, few if any of the 44,880 fans in attendance seemed to be complaining. Instead, a crackling sense of anticipation was moving through the stands at Jacobs Field, the neoclassical stadium that merged modern-day amenities with vintage ballpark aesthetics. The Indians and Florida Marlins had split the forgettable first two games of the Series, and had come back to Cleveland for Games 3, 4, and 5. And now, with the score still knotted at 7–7, the tension that is so much a part of postseason baseball was presenting itself.

Up in the NBC television booth, I felt hopeful. Though I had been critical of the wild-card system and new three-tiered playoff structure that had produced these two under-credentialed World Series opponents, I was rooting for both of these teams to prove themselves in some sense worthy.

The Indians had qualified for the Series despite posting the ninth-best regular-season record in the majors. They were probably the least impressive edition of the string of Cleveland contenders in the '90s.

The Marlins weren't so much mediocre as fabricated, a pure product of the times. Five years old, with an owner who had no background in baseball, they were an expansion team turned into a contender thanks to a $100 mil-

lion off-season investment and the wiles of manager Jim
Leyland, rescued from the financially overmatched Pittsburgh Pirates. The Marlins made the playoffs as a wild
card just weeks after owner Wayne Huizenga announced
that losses of $30 million would force him to put the
team on the market. They played baseball in a charmless
football stadium, and they'd sold their foul poles to an
office-supply store, which painted them to resemble
giant pencils. What more could you say? In an age when
it seemed that every expansion team incorporated teal or
black into its color scheme, the Marlins used both. They
were—as I'd been saying for weeks—the real team of the
'90s. And as it happened, they'd be dismantled before the
confetti from their victory parade could be swept away.

The matchup was not the stuff that programming
executives dream of. Television ratings were already in
the tank, the worst ever for a World Series to that point.
Don Ohlmeyer, the head of NBC's West Coast division
and the former executive producer of NBC Sports, had
done his part to put everyone in the proper Fall Classic
mood by publicly saying on the eve of the first game that
nothing would make him happier than to give the coverage to another network. "If the A&E channel called, I'd
take the call," said Ohlmeyer.

It wasn't just Don. Baseball-bashing was in full force,
much of it for good reason. The participants were undis-
tinguished, the first two games nondescript. Now Game
3, a World Series game, was being played under condi-

tions so ill-suited to baseball that if they presented themselves in April, the game would likely be postponed and rescheduled as part of an August doubleheader.

Still, as Cleveland's Eric Plunk threw the first pitch of the ninth to Bobby Bonilla, it was possible to forget all that. The game, while not artful, had been absorbing. Gary Sheffield was shaping up as the hero, having hit a home run in the first to put the Marlins ahead, then making a dazzling catch against the wall to end the seventh inning and preserve the 7–7 tie. The sheer tension of October baseball had at least temporarily transcended the game's problems, and the promise of a stirring finish was in the air.

And then it wasn't.

Just as baseball provides drama when you least expect it, it also can deny drama when you *most* expect it. And that's exactly what happened in the Inning That Wouldn't End. The top of the ninth lasted 34 minutes and featured seven Marlin runs, assembled through an unsightly collection of four singles, three walks, three errors, and a wild pitch.

As the temperature continued to drop and a game that had started at the ridiculous hour of 8:24 P.M. Eastern Standard Time pushed past midnight, the stultifying inning plodded forward. Along the way, it got much later and much colder.

"Everybody is leaving," said the NBC stage manager in the booth. "I wish we could too."

I wasn't sure if the rattling noise I kept hearing was the chattering of my colleagues' teeth, or merely the sound of people across the country wearily clicking their TV sets off as the now-listless game moved into its fifth hour.

Somewhere past midnight, during the commercial break accompanying yet another pitching change, my partner Bob Uecker stared out into the night and said to no one in particular, "This game sucks!"

I had to hand it to Ueck: It was the perfect summation of what was happening here. And once the top of the ninth was over, it didn't end there. Robb Nen came in with the seven-run lead and proceeded to nibble corners as though the tying run were at second, which, ultimately, it almost was.

The Indians would score four, leave one, and come within one baserunner of bringing the tying run to the plate—at 12:35 A.M. By then, nearly every aspect of this game made a mockery of the term "Fall Classic." Which is not to say that some of it wasn't perversely entertaining. As pitching coach Larry Rothschild visited the mound after Nen's third walk of the inning, Uecker asked what he might be telling the right-hander. I ventured a guess: "He's saying, 'I think room service closes at one A.M.; would you please get us out of here so I can have that bowl of soup!?'"

I'll admit it: At that point, I was just looking forward to getting off the air, before we had to send a St. Bernard with provisions of brandy and blankets to Jim Leyland's

84-year-old mother, encamped in the visitors' seats and as stoically determined to stick it out as we were.

She seemed emblematic of baseball fans in the late '90s: still there, gamely hanging on out of loyalty, memory, and sheer faith. Long after baseball itself had ceased to care much about any of that.

But baseball is, above all else, resilient. The game itself can be much better than those who run it. In '97, those who hung in there would witness a riveting Game 7 that unfolded like the final scenes of a good whodunit—after all those hundreds of games and all those thousands of innings, not even the normal nine was enough to bring it to resolution. It could end in a flash or go on indefinitely, and in the back-and-forth struggle of these two teams, in the solid-rock jaw of Indians manager Mike Hargrove and the edgy intensity of Marlins skipper Jim Leyland, in all those seasons these two baseball men had spent trying to get to this moment, you could at last feel the pull of something special.

The same pull could be felt September 8, 1998, when Mark McGwire homered his way into baseball history, with Roger Maris's family in the stands, and his competitor and compatriot Sammy Sosa out in the field. Or in the superb Game 5 battle between the Braves and Mets in the National League Championship Series in 1999.

That pull, unique in each particular, but ultimately familiar, is what baseball is all about.

And it is for moments like this that we keep returning to the game, why we still—despite all the evidence—hold out hope for it. Because we know that, at its core, the game itself can still reward us. That's why it's worth caring about. That's why it's worth arguing about.

And that's why I'm writing this book.

Now, before I go any farther, I need to correct one popular misconception, if only because it bears upon the case I'm about to make. Whenever I have written or spoken about baseball—whether arguing against an ill-advised change in the game, or arguing for an inspired one—I invariably wind up being described by detractors and admirers alike as a "traditionalist."

So let me now, once and for all, reject any simplistic characterization of me as a baseball traditionalist, purist, or incurable romantic. These labels are routinely slapped on all those who, for whatever reason, oppose any of the misguided changes that baseball has made in recent years. It has become a rhetorical crutch for those who espouse things like wild cards or radical realignment. It is so much easier to dismiss critics of these moves as dewy-eyed purists than it is to actually argue the merits of the point under discussion.

There *are* purists and over-the-top romantics in baseball, of course. There's a group of adults who are almost literally enchanted with the game, who see it as a parable, a metaphor for life, a prism through which to view the culture. It was Jacques Barzun who once said, "Whoever wants to know the heart and mind of America had better learn baseball," and all I can say, really, is that Jacques Barzun scares me a little bit.

Now, I will certainly cop to holding some of baseball's traditions in high esteem. And I do believe there's a beauty and a certain romance to the game, a richness of history that other sports cannot match. But one can appreciate those things without drowning in sentimentality, or viewing the sport as a sacred institution that should be worshiped rather than watched. This hushed, reverent, emerald greensward view of baseball is fine, in small doses, but for the most part it wasn't the way I was raised with the game, and isn't how I view it today.

In short, I'm a *Bull Durham* guy, not a *Field of Dreams* guy. I grew up with an inveterate gambler father who would curse even my beloved Mickey Mantle if he cost him a bet. I learned about baseball reading the likes of flinty, sardonic columnists like Dick Young, whose view of the essence of the game is not often confused with those who get choked up reading the infield fly rule. I rode the subways to Yankee Stadium, and saw and heard many things. But not "If you build it, they will come."

Yet the labels remain, partly because our image-driven culture seems to need them. So much of popular discourse these days has to be simple, has to fit a sound bite or a caricature. In certain quarters (and, sadly, throughout most of television), complexity itself is viewed as a nuisance. If you can't say something in 15 seconds, they don't want you to say it at all.

But there are certain points that are not easily made during the time it takes for the pitcher to go to the rosin bag. And I've learned that calling a ball game is not the time for an extended examination of baseball's economics, or all the ways that the wild card alters our perception of the regular season. This book, then, is my chance to lay it all out.

This isn't a commentator's diatribe against the sport, but rather a fan's case *for* baseball. What do I want? I think the same thing most baseball fans want: To see the game prove worthy of our devotion. To watch it move forward into the next century, while retaining the essence of what made it so worthwhile in the last one.

And to see baseball become fun again. That doesn't mean returning to eight-team leagues and flannel uniforms. It *does* mean leveling the playing field so all teams have a fighting chance, and returning some financial sanity to the game, so the teams themselves are something more than revolving doors for millionaires.

It means drawing distinctions between real progress

and mere change. It means reaching sensible conclusions about which aspects of the game should be preserved, which should be modified, and which should be overhauled.

I don't presume to have all the right answers. But I hope in many cases I'm on the right track. And at the very least, these things are worth discussing. That discussion should help us arrive at better answers than the ones we've been getting lately.

1

1993:
WHAT SHOULD HAVE
HAPPENED

It's easy to be lulled into thinking that everything's fine with baseball, because the moments that everyone remembers are still accumulating, as galvanizing as ever. Mark McGwire and Sammy Sosa chasing the home-run record, the mounting tension of the Mets–Braves National League Championship Series in '99, the all-the-chips-on-the-table drama of the seventh game of any World Series: These moments can still grip serious and casual fans alike. But beneath those surface highlights, the foundation of the sport is crumbling.

So the first thing you have to understand, if you're trying to figure out how to fix baseball, is how long it's been broken. On Opening Day 2000, the sport will begin its seventh season as an essentially dysfunctional operation.

Money is not just running the game, but whipping it: All eight teams that made the playoffs in 1999 had payrolls among the top ten in the majors. Player movement is at an all-time high, and the salary structure is spiraling further out of control. With every season, there seem to be more teams greeting Opening Day with little or no chance to compete for a pennant.

There's a feeling among large sectors of the press that certain fundamental inequities are a given, that baseball is always in some sort of dire straits, or always beset with economic injustice. And whenever someone points out that the situation need not be so bad, or the inequities quite so extreme, they treat such talk as a nostalgic, utopian formulation. And yet what are we really talking about? We're talking about *1993.* Not 1953. Not even 1973. 1993. Whatever has gone out of whack about baseball over the last 25 years, the vast majority has happened over the last seven.

What was baseball like way back in '93? No wild cards. No interleague play. No extra tier of playoffs. No minidivisions. Two seven-team divisions in each league.

And record-breaking attendance. The merits of the changes baseball then undertook can be debated. But the idea that they *had* to happen, based on some widespread public dissatisfaction with baseball as it then existed, is demonstrably false. Sure, baseball had its share of economic problems in 1993. It did *not* have seemingly insoluble structural and competitive problems in 1993. That was the ideal time for thoughtful change.

But the sport has only made its own circumstances worse since then. So before anything, let's retrace our steps and survey the wreckage.

Even in the early '90s, there were rumblings that baseball would move to an expanded playoff system, largely in response to lower television ratings, and with the awareness everywhere that the four-year, billion-dollar deal CBS had signed in 1989 had turned out to be a bust for the network, while unleashing a salary explosion within the game that outran the gains from the rights fees themselves. Ratings for the League Championship Series had dropped significantly, and World Series ratings were flagging as well. In the 1980s, five World Series had scored overall Nielsen ratings of 25 or higher, spectacular successes by any measure. But that plateau had not been achieved since. Such a drop could have been seen as cause for grave concern, or it could have been taken for what it was: a sign that people, with more choices than ever on cable, weren't watching the World Series as much as they used to, but were still watching in mammoth numbers, by the tens of millions. Next to the Super Bowl, the World Series remained the most popular annual televised sporting event in the country, and nothing else had even approached it, either in peak performance or sustained average.

And TV ratings aside, the crucial indicators of the game's popularity remained bright. In 1993 attendance went past 70 million, breaking the old record by 24 percent (the ninth record campaign in 12 years). Expansion teams in Colorado and Florida accounted for some of that increase, but even without those teams, the existing major league clubs would have broken the record. Six teams set attendance records that year. Minor league attendance, in its own way an even better barometer of how fans felt about the *game* of baseball, was up 10 percent to 30 million.

The '93 All-Star Game was held at Camden Yards in Baltimore, showcasing for an entire nation the appeal of an old-style park with modern-day conveniences. There was something alluring about this park, not because it presented some nostalgic homage to the past, but because it marked a return to the scale and feeling of intimacy in the game that had long been a big part of its appeal. Young stars who truly evoked the great names of the past were everywhere—Ken Griffey Jr., Barry Bonds, Mike Piazza.

And over the second half, baseball fans were treated to one of the great pennant races of the modern era— Giants and Braves down to the wire in the NL West—and then a stirring postseason, capped by Joe Carter's World Series–winning homer.

And so this was baseball in 1993: two divisions in each league, no wild cards, no interleague play, no "divisional playoff" series, no realignment (radical or otherwise). Absent the gimmickry and purposeless changes that would soon beset it, the game was in most ways aesthetically compelling and revenues were booming.

A distinction should be made here: Though the game was growing, it was not particularly healthy. Because of skyrocketing salaries, and because of the economic disparities apparent even then between small- and large-market teams, the game had serious financial problems. But a massive base of support was clearly there. Any business in America would have been lucky to have such a base, so the idea of the *game* of baseball as some critical patient requiring emergency surgery was absurd.

And yet throughout that season, a state of crisis pervaded the sport. Partly this was due to the well-founded fear that the owners and players would not be able to reach a collective bargaining agreement. But it was also brought on by a crisis of confidence. There was a perception in both sports and media circles that baseball, already trailing football, was about to be surpassed by basketball in overall popularity. That Michael Jordan was playing the hot sport of the future and that the staid game of baseball—with no dunking mascots, no laser shows, no gyrating dance teams, without even a shot clock—was history.

But a closer look reveals how mistaken that perception was. In terms of Nielsen ratings (at 17.3), the '93 Series between the Blue Jays and Phillies was an all-time low, excluding the earthquake-interrupted series of '89. This was partly due to the gradual attrition of the audience for almost all network programming, big event or otherwise. But it was also a function of geography. In any Series, viewership increases across the country and spikes to off-the-chart ratings shares in the two competing cities. But with Toronto as one of the participants, the Nielsens inevitably suffered, since all those viewers in Toronto and throughout Canada didn't figure in the Nielsen numbers. Those viewers affected the U.S. ratings the same as whoever picked the games up on satellite in Bangkok.

But even with all that working against baseball, the Series ratings were *virtually identical* to what was then the highest-rated NBA Finals ever, which also took place in 1993 and also went six games, with some powerful factors working in its favor. The Bulls were the reigning champions, facing the Phoenix Suns and the charismatic Charles Barkley in his MVP season. The whole league had been lifted by years of intense and skillful marketing, the Dream

Team's triumphant march through Barcelona the previous summer, and the Bulls' emerging dynasty. By then, Michael Jordan had reached a level of public celebration greater than that of Larry Bird or Magic Johnson, and had made the Bulls America's team in the process. And yet with all these factors and more, baseball's worst performance ever was roughly equal to basketball's best performance ever.

So here was baseball, with problems, yes, but with an essential product that clearly appealed to a wide cross-section of fans. A game whose tradition and stability should have been seen as distinctive characteristics and enduring strengths, yet in a position to change and innovate thoughtfully, reshaping the sport without distorting its essence. And that was the precise moment when the owners panicked, and began tearing their game—check that, *our* game—apart.

What the owners should have done back in 1993 was simple. As I argued then, that was the time to present—to both the Major League Baseball Players Association and the fans—a plan for baseball in the 21st century. Such a presentation would have, first and foremost, called for comprehensive revenue sharing among the owners, to address if not remedy the small-market/big-market inequities that were becoming obvious. (This was hardly visionary—Pete Rozelle had formalized the concept in the NFL more than three decades earlier.)

With revenue sharing in place, the owners then could have credibly presented a blueprint for baseball's long-term future. This would have included:

• The promise of some expansion, perhaps by two to four teams in coming years. Franchises in Colorado and Florida were set to begin play in 1994, bringing baseball to 28 teams. But the possibility of more teams, and thus more jobs for the Players Association, could have been used as a carrot in collective bargaining.

• In the collective bargaining agreement, there should have been something along the lines of what the NBA eventually came up with: a guaranteed minimum percentage of the gross for the players as a whole, a salary cap per team, a "superstar salary cap" at a very generous level, a salary *floor* per team, higher minimum salaries per player, and liberalized free agency accompanied by the elimination of arbitration as we now know it. All that should have been accompanied by incentives built into the system for the pie to grow—so that if the system worked, the owners would be happy to see the superstar salary ceiling in the next deal go from, say, $8 million to $10 million or $12 million or $15 million.

With all this on the table, the owners would then be in the position to say, truthfully and convincingly, "We are asking our most well-heeled member owners to alter their circumstances, and sacrifice to a much greater extent than we are asking any superstar player or the Players Association itself. But none of this flies without the players' cooperation in partnership."

• The owners should also have offered a blueprint for sensible divisional realignments and thoughtful reworkings of the schedule and postseason formats. This would have provided the game with a workable competitive structure that could hold for decades to come.

Armed with this package of proposals, the owners should have asked for, or purchased, time on ESPN to make a kind of "State of the Game Address." There, a capable and credible spokesman might have said, "What we are offering is a vision of baseball which retains its enduring principles but which modernizes for the next century. This is where we ask the players to go with us."

This statement of principles and objectives would have served notice that the owners had (1) a creative and workable plan for addressing the game's problems, (2) sound ideas for how the game should develop into the future, and (3) a different kind of resolve, one marked by having a better and more reasonable argument than the Players Association. The owners had said the game was broken in the past, but for the first time their case would have been fueled by something more than mere anger and complaint. For the first time, an objective person would have been forced to conclude that the owners had presented a logical and coherent case for positive change.

The televised address, which could have been made on the eve of spring training 1994, might have included this message: "The players have the right to strike anytime during this season, but we implore them not to and we call their attention, as well as the public's, to the fact that there need not be a single game missed in 1994. Even if the players disagree with some of our suggestions, we're open to negotiation. We have a full year now to negotiate. The players can strike on Opening Day, on July the first, on September first. We urge them not to. If a single baseball game is missed this year, it's because the players have decided they don't want to talk anymore.

"But we will also tell you this: If there is not a substantial change in the way baseball operates, we will not open up again in 1995. There will not be an Opening Day in 1995 and there will not be a season at all until we reach a reasonable conclusion. We don't want that to happen. And if the players come anywhere close to what we're talking about, it won't happen."

I realize that, even if this entire plan were presented, the players likely would have gone on strike anyway, because they're intractable and too ideological and they didn't believe that the owners had sufficient resolve. It turned out the owners *did* have sufficient resolve; they just didn't have an intelligent and honest plan—which was ultimately a fatal flaw.

But, returning to the scenario, if the owners had indeed put such a plan forth, suppose the players did go on strike. The owners, for the first time, would have owned the high ground.

And their acting commissioner would have been in a position to say, "You know what folks? We're not tied to any of the owners' mistakes of the past. Over the history of baseball's labor relations, the players have been right. But they're not right anymore. We are not looking to take back from them any of their hard- and justly-won gains. We're looking for a new paradigm for baseball as the 21st century approaches. We think this is tremendously reasonable. We're willing to modify it or change it if they've got any better ideas. But if they don't come a long way in the direction we're talking about, there's no point in playing baseball in 1995."

A 1994 strike by the players then still would have cost the sport Tony Gwynn's run at .400, Matt Williams's or Ken Griffey's run at Roger Maris, and, as it turned out, the 1994 World Series. Such a strike still would have been foolish and self-defeating. The fans still would have been angry and disillusioned. But here's the crucial difference: At that point, it would have been pretty clear whom they should have been angry at.

It would have been just as clear that owners who had publicly stated they were willing to lose part or all of the 1995 season certainly weren't going to capitulate in an *off*-season after a lost World Series. They would have already taken the best hit the players could have delivered. The leverage would have shifted almost completely to the owners. (Some thought that despite the owners' clumsiness, the leverage *had* shifted in their favor anyway by early '95. But the plan to use replacement players and other tactical errors diminished their already question-able position, and ultimately they were undone by Don Fehr's end run to the courts.)

With public support on their side, the owners' willing-ness to continue the fight would only have grown, while the players—faced with continued lost wages and the pub-lic's scorn—would have eventually had to sign on to some-thing close to what they were offered in the first place.

This would have meant a victory not only for the own-ers, but for baseball and its fans. And, in a real sense, for the players themselves, whether they realized it at first or not.

2

1993:

WHAT DID HAPPEN

Now back to reality.

Baseball did none of these things, exhibited no vision whatsoever. There was no consensus, no agreement, no coherent plan.

The owners, of course, couldn't even agree on what to order for lunch. They didn't come together—and had nothing to come together over in the first place, beyond the vague relic of this inherited antipathy toward the

Players Association. Instead, in the 12 months leading up to Opening Day 1994, the caretakers of the game dashed around willy-nilly and announced the following:

• That in 1994 there would be three divisions in each league, though still playing a balanced schedule. Which meant that the "division winners" would be all the more arbitrary, since all teams were playing virtually the same schedule.

• A wild-card playoff spot in each league, given to the non-division winner with the best record, which automatically rendered an all-or-nothing race of sustained excellence (like 1993's San Francisco–Atlanta thriller) fundamentally impossible.

• A revenue-sharing plan (involving the transfer of funds from the richest to poorest teams), which the owners themselves dubbed significant to the point of being revolutionary, when in fact it was woefully inadequate and unconnected to any comprehensive principle. No objective observer believed that this would do anything much to correct baseball's problem of competitive imbalance.

• An abomination called The Baseball Network, in which Major League Baseball itself would no longer receive rights fees from the networks broadcasting its games, but would instead recoup its money by taking a large portion of ad revenues that were generated.

The real impact wasn't on the sport's finances but its

fans. An agreement had been reached whereby only the World Series, among all the games broadcast, would be telecast nationally. This was an unprecedented surrender of prestige, as well as a slap at all serious fans. For decades, one of the things that separated the Big Two from hockey and basketball was that all playoff games in both baseball and football had been nationally televised. But now the owners—and the networks—were telling America that (1) the public demanded more playoffs, and would get them, and yet (2) both the divisional series and the League Championship Series now merited scarcely higher priority than the regional coverage provided for a Big Ten football game between Wisconsin and Michigan.

• An "offer" to the Players Association—which finally came at the eleventh hour—pegged to the salary-cap idea the players have long viewed as anathema, but without any of the other elements that could make a salary cap in some form part of a convincing vision for an improved game.

So at a time when baseball fever was more than some mere advertising slogan, the owners effectively did their best to destroy the very soul of the game. Instead of defiantly accentuating the differences between baseball and other sports, celebrating its unique feel and rhythm, they tried to synch up their timeless game with what they thought was the prevailing zeitgeist, to model their game after the NBA. More playoff rounds. More screaming music in between innings. More flash and dash.

And all that, of course, served as a prelude for the sport's ultimate betrayal, the 1994 strike that led to the canceling of the World Series.

The owners clearly wished to provoke a strike, and did so. It was also just as clear they had no idea where the game should go, economically or competitively, or how it should get there. Those who propose that replacement players be used in games that will count in league standings, even after a strike is presumably settled, hardly win the confidence of thoughtful baseball fans. Hence, their position was not only no better than the players', it was worse—since no matter how unreasonable the players' position may sometimes be, it always has a certain baseline integrity. Throughout the strike, the players never allowed themselves to seem confused, illogical, or dishonest.

Forced to choose between the lesser of two evils, many informed members of the press sided with the players—as did federal judge Sonya Sotomayor, after concluding that the inconsistencies of the owners' approach amounted to bargaining in bad faith.

Unfortunately, work stoppages were not new in baseball. There had been eight of them in less than 25 years, but they had always been resolved before the postseason.

Until the Strike of '94.

The worst part about the strike, and the part that still reverberates today, is that it finally forced many fans to conclude that the owners and the players had little but contempt for the game of baseball, saw it largely as a moneymaking instrument. It seemed that the fondness and enduring connection that fans across America felt for the game wasn't shared by those who ran and played it. Whether or not this was entirely true, it was the overwhelming perception—a perception that lingers today.

By the time the sad press conferences announcing the cancellation of the season were played out in the fall of '94, most fans didn't even feel disgust, which at least would have been a passionate and active emotion, but something much sadder as far as the game was concerned: apathy. How could they feel any other way after watching the very caretakers of the game treat it with such disregard? The public reaction was logical and painfully predictable: If they don't care enough to save the season, why should we?

The impact was brutal and long-lasting, and not even the McGwire-Sosa summer of '98 could truly change it. As Leonard Koppett so aptly describes the fallout in his *Concise History of Major League Baseball,* "Two fundamental changes would occur that could not be undone or ignored. The inviolable connection to the past would be broken, and the separation of baseball business from baseball on the field would no longer be possible in the consciousness of anyone thinking about it, especially those not involved in the business. The second was even

more important than the first. The perception of baseball's romance as distinct from its business operations
was permanently tarnished if not totally erased."

Eventually, inevitably, the game returned. But it felt
fundamentally different. While millions claimed they'd
never come back, millions more still wanted to care but
encountered a game and product far less worthy of their
devotion.

And by the time baseball reached its first postseason
in two years, its first trip to the brave new world of wild
cards, divisional series, and The Baseball Network, the
depressing truth was undeniable. Almost all decisions
concerning the game were based on short-term revenue
grabs rather than enduring baseball principles.

As ludicrous as The Baseball Network was, it should
have been far less troublesome to real fans than the concept of the wild card. The wild card corrupted both the
pennant race and the postseason. The Baseball Network
was idiotic, but it was just a television idiocy. It didn't
fundamentally corrupt the game (except, of course, in
the sense that for their steadfast, spaniel-like loyalty, the
most impassioned fans in baseball were now prevented
from watching many of the playoff games they wanted
to see).

So after that one-season calamity, The Baseball Network was junked, but baseball's pattern of haphazard
changes persisted. After catching their breath in 1996,
the owners threw in another piecemeal change for 1997:

• Interleague play. While regular-season games between the leagues might diminish the mystique of the World Series, it remained an idea, on balance, whose time had come. But it came without any sort of thoughtful plan for how it would be implemented or cycled. The NFL plays interconference games with an unbalanced schedule—half of each team's games are within the division—and schedules interconference games on a fixed cycle, so a division is matched against each of the other conference's three divisions once every three years. No such stipulation was made by baseball. Which meant that one of the main appeals of interleague play—allowing fans in, say, Pittsburgh, to see Ivan Rodriguez—would be denied, not just that year or next, but perpetually.

At first, though, bolstered by the sheer novelty and by natural rivalries like Mets–Yankees, Rangers–Astros, and Cubs–White Sox, interleague play looked on the surface like a hit, boosting attendance numbers and increasing fan interest.

But at the same time, it was fueling something dangerous and potentially disastrous. Baseball was so anxious to declare something, anything, a success, that it overstated the true value of the novelty of interleague play, and used it to make an earnest, impassioned case for:

• Radical realignment. This was, in many ways, baseball's single most irrational impulse of the entire decade. Try to follow the tortured logic: Interleague play between neighboring teams is a success, so let's have radical realignment, reorganizing the leagues along purely geographical lines. So we will scrap the century-old distinction between the American and National Leagues, and now the Phillies and Giants can be an "interleague game." Here we have struck some new note of bizarre cognitive dissonance.

While all this directionless dickering was going on, the Florida Marlins won the World Series in 1997. About 10 minutes after doing so, Marlins owner Wayne Huizenga almost literally cashed in his chips. He cleared out his best players so fast you'd have thought they were overdue video rentals. There were barely any veteran Marlins around on Opening Day 1998 to collect their rings. In 1994, baseball had no champion. In 1998, it effectively had no defending champion.

This was partly the product of crass opportunism, and partly the result of the disastrous new economy of baseball in the late '90s. And by this point, it had become clear just how badly the owners had lost, again, in the latest strike.

Of course, the owners had been crying poor since John McGraw was a lad. Their claims should always be viewed skeptically. Still the evidence mounted, evidence that said baseball needed economic reform. Not for the owners' sake—for the game's sake.

Small-market teams were over a barrel. Instead of

big-market clubs having payrolls twice as large as their small-market competitors, it was not uncommon for the biggest payrolls to be five times as large as the smallest, and twice as large as the payrolls of what now passed for middle-market teams.

Plus, with Camden Yards showing the way, and Jacobs Field, Coors Field, and others following suit, several franchises had new ballparks that were cash cows, further exaggerating the income disparity between franchises. In some cases, those new parks were in markets that also had huge, exponential advantages in local broadcast revenue. Now these factors combined, and what were once differences of degree exploded into fundamental and unbridgeable differences of kind.

With these new revenue streams for the richest teams, the salary structure spiraled anew. While the Expos might have been harder-pressed to pay Larry Walker $3 million instead of $2.3, suddenly they were looking at having to pay him $8 million. And the team that, through masterful managing and a superb farm system, had somehow achieved the best record in baseball at the strike of '94, became a franchise that by 1996 had absolutely no chance to compete.

Faced with these dizzying changes, the sports media did not serve fans well. The center couldn't hold, and any consensus that might have existed about what the sport did or didn't stand for, where it should or shouldn't be going, was lost. And in the void, a thousand crackpot opinions sprang up, from graduates of the Ready-Fire-Aim school of analysis. Major national publications put forth ideas as addled as proposing that baseball separate into divisions based on revenues. Others insisted that baseball must realign geographically so that the Mets and Yankees, and the Cubs and White Sox, could play each other a dozen times every year. Or that the next expansion include realignment into eight four-team divisions, to create more races. (Why stop there? Why not sixteen twos? By this logic, that would be twice as exciting.)

Other commentators, perhaps having grown fed up with the whole thing, and wishing to simply enjoy what was left of a badly mangled game, chose to accept the current situation as just so much business as usual, characterizing objections to it as myopic. When my friend, the normally astute Keith Olbermann, argues that certain dominant teams and dynasties have never been bad for sports, he misses a crucial point. No one ever said those teams had to be the Yankees or had to be the Braves. Prior to the skewed economics of late-'90s baseball, dynasties weren't predestined. How do you explain the Big Red Machine or the Oakland A's dynasty, both in small markets? The point is that while the larger-market teams may always have had certain advantages, they were not always perceived to have a monopoly on sustained success.

And this can be illustrated most dramatically by looking at what happened in baseball during the first 15 years of free agency. Despite the wailings of Chicken Little types, free agency—at least at first—actually enhanced competitive balance, improved the game, added some excitement and life to it. During that period of time, did the Yankees win? Did the Dodgers win? Yes and yes. But Cincinnati also was a dominant team, and Kansas City was a perennial power, one of the strongest teams in baseball for more than a decade. The Oakland A's won three straight pennants between 1988 and 1990. The Minnesota Twins, now on baseball's endangered-species list, were world champions in 1987 and 1991. The Pittsburgh Pirates won three straight division titles in the early '90s, when winning a division really meant something.

But by 1994 or 1995 Pittsburgh was being talked about as a baseball wasteland, and the Bonds-Bonilla Bucs seemed as far removed from the present reality as Willie Stargell's Pirates or, for that matter, Bill Mazeroski's Pirates. But it's in the past *decade* that Cincinnati won the World Series. That Oakland was baseball's best team. That Montreal had the best record in baseball at the time of the strike. That the Twins won their second World Series in a four-year span. Suddenly, none of these developments are remotely possible, all due exclusively to economics.

This isn't just an evolution; it's a shift of fundamental proportions.

Which brings us pretty much up to date: The owners still disorganized. The fans still there, in some capacity, but not with the connection or loyalty they've shown in the past. And the Players Association still blithely arguing that there is enough profit for everyone, and that any change in the present system is tantamount to an assault on the sacred concept of the American free market. And on the field, the game itself has been ripped from its moorings.

Baseball is broken, and it's up to Major League Baseball—the Commissioner's Office and the owners, who are collectively the caretakers of the game—to fix it.

The arguments of those who would keep the status quo fall flat. People say, "Baseball has always been a business," as though that statement, alone, says something meaningful. But to tell the full story, the point needs to be made that until recently, baseball has never been *only* a business.

Baseball has to change, for a couple of reasons. For one, in a number of markets it can't sustain, let alone build, popularity in the present environment. Other economies that go off the rails have course corrections. But that would be particularly dangerous in baseball, because if you wait until teams start going out of business, you're facing the possibility that good baseball towns—cities with histories of fan support, like Kansas City and Minnesota—will lose franchises.

The second reason is that this game, as it's conducted today, has lost much of its appeal. When a fan has to make abstruse financial calculations about multimedia conglomerates just to gauge his team's prospects, when the rosters of even the strongest teams are constantly shuffling, making Major League Baseball feel like a giant rotisserie league, we have gone way off course.

By early 2000, baseball was preparing to address these problems, at least in some fashion. Commissioner Bud Selig has been given expanded powers to deal with issues such as revenue inequities. The question is exactly what course of action will baseball take? It's one thing to identify a problem, quite another to arrive at a solution. And as we've seen over the last decade, baseball's leaders have often shown an uncanny ability to make the wrong choices from among a number of options.

The first step will be crucial, because before we can suggest fixes, we need to define the problems, give some thought to what baseball should be, and explain what we're trying to accomplish. We have to regain some sense of critical consensus, some common ground from which we can map baseball's future. This is a basic, perhaps even a remedial, exercise. But at this point, it has become a necessary first step to addressing each problem.

3

THE NATURE OF
SPORTS LEAGUES

*"We've reached the point where the first duty of
intelligent men is to restate the obvious."*

— GEORGE ORWELL

Major League Baseball
is a special kind of business. There are 30 owners who
are at once fiercely independent and competitive, yet
each is dependent on all the others for success. While
baseball is a confederation of private enterprises, it occu-
pies a quasi-public position. The things that make sports
more than mere entertainment—the way a team repre-
sents a city to the rest of the country and often the world;

the fact that sports are one of the few areas of common ground left in an increasingly splintered society—these factors are independent of the narrow, reductionist view of sports as business.

So we have to start here, we have to restate the obvious, answer the most elemental questions. What is a league, anyway? Is it "just a business," as so many owners and players (and fans) insist? Or is it better understood as something beyond that?

The truth, of course, is that sports leagues transcend the boundaries of just about every conventional business. They are both private (the teams generally keep the profits and take the losses) and public (the teams are often playing in publicly financed stadiums, on public property). Owners are by and large private professionals who don't have to open their books up to anyone, and yet much of their business—broadcast revenues, every player's salary— is a matter of public record. The employees are uniquely blessed (name another industry in which the *average* employee is a millionaire) and uniquely constricted (how many millionaires have to move to a different town and company at the whim of their bosses?).

Yet some big-market owners would like us to believe that Major League Baseball is like 30 restaurants on a busy street, and that each owner has no real concern about the success of the other 29.

But properly understood, Major League Baseball is less like 30 different restaurants and much more like 30 *franchises within a single restaurant chain.* They're competitive, they all want profits and the prestige of a five-star rating, but they're not trying to put each other out of business. None can survive without the others. Leagues are, in the words of Notre Dame economist Richard Sheehan, a "joint effort," with all franchises needing to cooperate in some measure to generate revenues.

The big-market owners aren't the only ones whose view of leagues is self-serving. Mention the idea of a salary cap—or even connecting salaries to a percentage of gross revenues—and Don Fehr becomes Steve Forbes, waving the capitalist flag for all he's worth. The mere thought that anyone would suggest that—for purposes of competitive balance—there should be some kind of upward limit on salaries or team payrolls sends the officers of the Players Association scurrying for the barricades. This is the one principle that is inviolate, the one they claim they would sacrifice a year or more of their careers to protect.

If old-timers don't get a break on pensions, if baseball installs a playoff system that cheapens both the regular season and the postseason, if the sport continues to lag in minority hiring, if artificial turf blights the game and shortens careers, if we play in a league where two-thirds of us are consigned to teams that have no real chance to win, all those things are less important than whether Shawn Green can make $12 million instead of $9 million. *There's* an issue the players will go to war over.

Yet the first moment Marvin Miller and the Players

Association had a chance for completely unfettered capitalism—the moment when the Players Association could elect to have all players declared free agents, in 1976—he actually argued against it. He realized that limiting the supply of player availability (of having fewer free agents available per season) would drastically increase the demand. And he was right (ask Wayne Garland).

Miller understood, though he might be reluctant to say so today, that some controls are required and appropriate in sports, and would (in this case) ultimately benefit the players.

In fact, one could cite many examples of how basic operating principles of a league differ from a typical American business in a free-market economy:

• If a league were anything like a true free market, it would be unthinkable for teams to share revenue even to the extent that they share it now. Unthinkable to pool network television revenue. Unthinkable to pool merchandising revenue. Unthinkable to install—and this is done with the players' approval, by the way—a luxury tax.

• If we were really interested in a pure free market, would we allow players to be traded for each other? Can Sony deal Bob Dylan to Virgin Records for the Rolling Stones? Can Delta swap three pilots to TWA for two flight attendants, four skycaps, and a ticket agent to be named later? And yet trades, and even straight player *sales,* are a given in sports.

• Where but in a league is there a draft of talent? Even though the draft varies in its particulars from sport to sport, the concept of the draft remains the same, with players belonging to an organization, an organization that then controls them to one extent or another—in the case of baseball, both in the minor leagues and for as long as six years at the major league level. That in and of itself is far more restrictive of freedom, and far more objectionable—if you think about it in terms of pure free-market economics—than a high-end limitation on someone who is already making an eight-figure salary.

• The idea of roster limitations. An analogy here is this: Can CBS tell NBC, "We only used 25 Olympic staffers in Nagano, so you can only use 25 in Sydney. We're competitors, aren't we?" Clearly ridiculous—anywhere but in sports, where the concept is essential. In fact, if the argument as it is glibly offered by the Players Association is "How are you going to tell a businessman how much he can spend to improve his product," then how can you arbitrarily limit his workforce? Wealthy teams would love to have a 15-man pitching staff. And why not three guys just to be pinch-runners?

• Where but in a sports league would you find the use of an expansion draft in which existing companies, if you will, formally take part in helping stock new companies?

• In sports, unlike other businesses, territorial rights have meaning. If Burger King wants to move across the street from McDonald's and take their chances, that's just a business judgment. The Kansas City Royals cannot decide tomorrow that they would be better off being the second most popular team in St. Louis than being the only team in Kansas City and just move in. It's unthinkable.

• In any other field, it would be normal, even desirable, for the weaker and less capable businesses to fall by the wayside, proof that the market was working itself out. But this is hardly a natural occurrence in pro sports, where a league is only as healthy as its weakest franchise, and where any team going under—and especially a pattern of failures—reflects poorly on a league's image, reputation, and overall health.

• In a league, all members compete for the same thing and seek the same ideal outcome. Not so in other businesses. A cozy café can do well on its own terms, without having to directly compete with the city's finest steakhouse. They both can thrive; they both can satisfy their customers while delivering a different dining experience. Customers enter each establishment with appropriately different expectations. But the Pittsburgh Pirates can't decide to tell their fans that they intend to *perpetually* serve them a fifth-place product and that the team should not be judged in relation to what teams in other cities are putting on the field. Other businesses are about finding a niche, but in sports leagues, every team is striving for the same niche—the one on the top of the heap. Their customers must believe that they have a chance, at least once in a while, to get there.

• In baseball, as in other sports, the only lasting definition of success comes on the field. Forced to choose between winning a championship and breaking even, or not winning a title but turning a profit, almost any owner—save for the most craven and soulless—would choose the former over the latter. In a heartbeat. Baseball fans know the Detroit Tigers won the World Series in 1984. But which was the most profitable team in baseball that year? No fan knows, and even better, no fan cares.

Sports' equivalent of the *Fortune* 500 appears engraved in gold on its trophies. Winning matters. And while any business must show a regular profit to survive over the long term, profit is not baseball's only bottom line.

What's become increasingly clear, in the last quarter of the 20th century, is that players and owners need each other, need to sustain what economists sometimes refer to as the "natural monopoly" that is a successful major sports league.

It's also obvious that, with a sane economic system in place, this state of affairs helps both parties. Owners get a break—and players get more money—when a single league is recognized as the one legitimate context for the best of any particular team sport. In America, even the greatest players in team sports cannot market their talents outside the context of an established league. Though they can obviously make outside income (by the millions, in some cases), their recognizability and value relies on their involvement with the league. It's there that their performances have present and historical meaning. If every single player in the major leagues were instantly transported to a new "Players League," and tomorrow Mark McGwire were to bat against Randy Johnson, it wouldn't have anything like the same meaning, authenticity, or appeal. Although this is true of all team sports, it's even more true of baseball, because of the game's reliance on history.

Just as players aren't well-served by bolting to other leagues or functioning as freelance performers, an independent league can't profit from Ken Griffey's talents the way Major League Baseball can, simply because the majors already have more than a century's worth of infrastructure, through facilities, tradition, and media coverage.

By the same token, a scattering of leagues across the country wouldn't garner even a tiny fraction of the focus, the fan support, or the television dollars that a single league recognized as the best would. Only through this "natural monopoly" can baseball generate the sort of revenue that makes even fringe players millionaires.

Major League Baseball is indeed a monopoly, but this doesn't carry the sinister implications that it does in other realms, or once did in baseball before players' rights were established.

The Nature of Sports Leagues

A sports league is a business whose success and appeal to the public depend on both the quality of play and the perceived fairness of competition. It's a business in which the competitors must simultaneously be partners. For each of these partners, the primary goal, the desired end result, is performance in pursuit of the championship of that league.

When leagues are understood this way, a whole world opens up: This is how leagues work. Not in some utopian vision, but in the real world. Leagues have prospered this way; team histories and enduring fan loyalties have been built this way.

In this context, franchises still have an incentive both to make profits and to win championships, as well as an obligation to the welfare of the league as a whole. And since it is only within this context of a league that team-sports athletes receive maximum financial rewards and can achieve other career goals, they too bear a measure of responsibility for the overall well-being of the league. And that is why in a league, certain restraints and conditions that might be unacceptable elsewhere are not only permissible but desirable.

So, in this case, the ideal is at once practical and profitable. Teams make money. Players get rich. And fans get something that, in a real sense, money can't buy.

4

IT'S NOT THE REVENUE—IT'S THE REVENUE SHARING

There was a time, not long ago, when the Seattle Mariners looked like the glamour team of the future. Ken Griffey Jr. patrolled center field (and often the area just beyond it) and possessed the game's sweetest batting swing. The precocious Alex Rodriguez had the composure of a veteran, and a mix of power and speed nearly unique in a middle infielder. And Randy Johnson, the game's most intimidating pitcher, took the ball every fifth day, giving the Mariners a chance in any short series.

It seemed that all the Mariners lacked to become the team of the next decade was another revenue stream, in the form of a handsome new stadium that could guarantee them dollars to keep Seattle on a par with other upper-middle-market clubs. So the people of Seattle ponied up, and just after the '99 All-Star break, the gorgeous new Safeco Field opened.

Whereas the Kingdome had been soulless and claustrophobic, Safeco was a state-of-the-art retro ballpark, featuring the contours of classic stadium architecture mixed with all the amenities of a turn-of-the-century entertainment complex. And Seattle's fans, criticized for being blasé in the past, came out in droves. They sold out all 36 games after the All-Star break, drawing at a clip that would easily exceed three million for a full season.

But by then, Randy Johnson was long gone. And after the '99 season, Seattle's new GM, Pat Gillick, said the team would have to trade Griffey, and perhaps Rodriguez as well, because they couldn't afford to pay either player market value when they became free agents following the 2000 season. And even if they could, they'd find themselves in a double bind. Players like Griffey and Rodriguez are adamant about playing for a contender. They urge their teams to make a "commitment" to winning, and yet if the present market goes unchecked, retaining superstars at their market value will leave most teams without the necessary resources to build quality teams around them.

The Seattle case is just the most vivid example of an ongoing lesson about baseball economics. The problem in the sport is not a lack of revenue. There's plenty of it. Without significant reforms, however, it will never *seem* to be enough. The vast majority of teams will always be chasing additional revenues even after new stadiums have been built, new network contracts have been signed, and next year's ticket prices have been raised. The problem baseball faces is an insufficient amount of revenue sharing, along with a financial model that isn't sustainable.

Meanwhile, who are the NBA's defending champions? The San Antonio Spurs, that's who. And what do these cities have in common: Sacramento, Indianapolis, Salt Lake City? Not only do they all have NBA franchises, they all have *contending teams*. The mere thought of a major league baseball franchise in any of those markets is laughable. Not only couldn't they contend, they couldn't even survive. Yet the NBA has a financial model that, while imperfect, is certainly workable. Fans of every team—and just as important, players on each club—have reason to believe they have a chance to win, either now or, if things break right, in the future. All this accomplished without a single sighting of an NBA player holding a tin cup on a street corner.

Because so many other variables are beyond a league's control or are in constant flux—the respective sizes of cities and markets, attendance patterns, personnel development—leagues must share a significant amount of revenue to have a stable economic framework. The NFL learned these lessons long ago. Major League Baseball is still flunking remedial economics.

Sports is about beating your opponents, not destroying them. Not only do you need opponents to play the game in the first place, you need capable opponents to give the contest (whether single-game or season-long) credibility. And to achieve competitive balance, especially in this era, you have to have comprehensive revenue sharing. And once that's clear, then so is the corollary: Baseball's problem isn't that there is not enough *total* revenue, it's that the salary scale is way out of control, and the substantial existing revenue isn't distributed equitably.

There are three main revenue streams in major professional sports these days: the gate (ticket sales, including luxury boxes), broadcasting (national and local TV and radio broadcasting rights), and stadium revenue (parking, concessions, souvenirs, etc.). The most successful leagues share a significant portion of revenue, much more so than baseball does.

Here's where the sport lags behind:

• The gate. Where once visiting teams received a small amount of the gate (an 80/20 split in the American

League, something less than a dollar a head in the National), now there is no home/visitor split. Since the 1995 collective bargaining agreement, the gate has not been divided at all. With the exception of a small tax paid to the central office to cover league management expenses, home teams now keep 100 percent of their ticket sales, as compared to, for example, the NFL's 60/40 home-away split. The change in the '95 agreement was meant to be offset by the revenue-sharing plan that was instituted at that time. In fact, the smaller-market teams in the American League might have been better served by keeping or increasing the old 80/20 split.

• Broadcasting revenues. Between national TV contracts and the sale of MLB-licensed merchandise, each team in the majors receives about $15 million per year. But even when you include the national licensing shares, that figure makes up less than half of baseball's total revenue from broadcast sources.

The inequity arises in local radio and television revenues, where there's a gap of more than $50 million per year between the richest and poorest teams. That is the core of baseball's problem, and the revenue sharing and luxury tax pushed forward in the last deal doesn't come close to solving it. It is the financial equivalent of putting a Band-Aid on a bullet wound.

• Stadium revenue. Because stadium revenue and the means by which it is generated are the most independent aspects of the equation, it's not easily or appropriately split. We'll leave this subject alone. But it's worth noting that revenue disparity is great here also. In 1999, some franchises made as much as $30 million in stadium revenue alone, while others were bringing in less than $10 million. Which makes it all the more important that revenue be more equitably distributed in the other two areas.

I think it's safe to say that revenue (and the payroll disparity that inevitably comes with it) has become a problem when this factor—more than the previous season's record, more than management acumen, more than any other single factor in the game—becomes the biggest single indicator of a team's chances for success.

In fact, since the strike, there hasn't been a team that advanced to the World Series that didn't have one of the top 10 payrolls in the majors. And every single season, the world champion has had one of the top five payrolls in baseball.

In 1995, Atlanta (with the fourth-highest payroll) beat Cleveland (with the seventh-highest).

In 1996, the Yankees (first) topped the Braves (third).

In 1997, the Marlins (fifth) edged the Indians (third).

In 1998, the Yankees (second) swept the Padres (10th, at $53 million).

In 1999, the Yankees (first) swept the Braves (third).

Eight of the 10 World Series participants since the

strike have had payrolls among the top five in the majors that season. And in 1999, of course, the eight teams that made the playoffs were all among the top 10 payrolls in baseball.

Now let's kill some empty rhetoric right here: Every time a big-money ballclub like the Orioles or the Dodgers stinks up the joint, someone says that it "proves" that money isn't that important. But the question isn't whether big-money teams can fail. They can and do—and with only two spots in the World Series, it's inevitable that some big-money teams will fall short of the championship, while other mismanaged high-payroll teams will fail spectacularly (as they have since the dawn of free agency). But this doesn't prove anything except that money thrown at a problem doesn't necessarily solve the problem.

The proper question is this: Can teams succeed in the current environment *without* having a mammoth payroll? The answer, clearly, is no. Lower-payroll teams, like the Reds in '99, might get hot and challenge for a playoff spot every once in a while, but those teams aren't going to get to the World Series, much less win it. And just as tellingly, they cannot have sustained success at this level of play.

No, if you don't have a payroll of at least $50 million (and likely more in the near future), you don't have a chance to compete. As Sandy Alderson said before he left the A's to join Major League Baseball's central office, small-market teams are no longer in the business of competitive baseball, they're in the business of enter-tainment—because their knowledgeable fans *know* that these teams can't compete. So they have to get fans to the ballpark by some means other than the pursuit of a championship.

The problem is so acute, the situation so far off track, that to put it in perspective, it's helpful to think of it this way: If you were the Kansas City Royals and you were offered a deal that guaranteed you would have one egre-gious call against you every game, but you would get to have the same payroll as the Yankees, what do you think you'd do? You'd sign as soon as you could.

The fact is, the single biggest indicator of a team's opportunity for success from one year to the next is whether that team has a payroll among the top few teams in the league. Period.

This goes against what sports are supposed to be—and for the most part have been—about. In every game you've got, in every schoolyard game, the whole idea of picking sides is to make the game as even as possible to make it interesting.

I realize that at various times in its history baseball has faced significant economic inequities among its own-ers. We all know about Connie Mack selling off star play-ers to keep his Philadelphia A's afloat. Not all aspects of baseball's past deserve to be fondly remembered. But cit-ing historical precedents for an objectionable condition is hardly an argument for the return to or continuation of that condition. Especially when remedies are at hand.

Sports, more so than most other enterprises, are *designed* to be fair. Teams are supposed to begin, to the greatest degree possible, on a level playing field. (Thus the very cliché about equality of opportunity—the "level playing field"—comes from the sports world.) And for generations this has been an accepted tenet of sports. This is why an obviously blown call on a single play in a big game is talked about more than a decade later. Yet the difference wrought by one bad call by Don Denkinger is nothing like the competitive disadvantage that small-market (and these days even middle-market) teams face each season.

Now, that does not mean that every team has or should have an equal chance every year. In a normal sports environment, teams rise and fall over the long term, make their own chances and lose out on others, based on skill, perseverance, luck, or some combination of all these things.

If, through a run of outrageous fortune, adversities, blunders, front-office inanity, and other circumstances that make up their star-crossed condition, the Red Sox go 80-plus years without a world title or the Cubs go 50-plus without a pennant, that's part of baseball's lore. But if fans of the Kansas City Royals or Minnesota Twins feel they're doomed to spend decades out of contention simply because the deck is stacked against them (rather than the stars aligned against them), that's part of baseball's problem. And that's what's happened in the economic environment of the late '90s.

Opponents of comprehensive revenue sharing (who implicitly also oppose competitive balance) inevitably respond with the same tired mantra about free markets and capitalism. But to quote longtime Players Association ally—and friend to capitalists everywhere—George Will: "Sports leagues have rules to contrive competitive balance. The aim is not to guarantee teams equal revenues but revenues sufficient to give each team periodic chances of winning if each uses its revenues intelligently. Baseball's rules no longer suffice."

The structure of leagues has always evolved with adjustments being made to accommodate both fairness and shifting realities. If, for a large number of teams, their player-employees, and their fans, the realistic hope of achieving the ultimate goal of a championship ceases to exist, common sense and fairness dictate that a new paradigm must emerge. The modern ideal is a league in which all parties (owners and players) can flourish financially but only insofar as all franchises have a reasonable chance to compete. In short, it's time for new rules.

And the biggest one has to do with revenue inequity. I've said it before and I'll say it again: Baseball's problem isn't a lack of revenue. The sport generated *more than twice* as much revenue in 1999 as it did in 1990. And instead of economic inequity being reduced, it has grown markedly worse. Baseball would be better off with flat revenues and a sound economic system than with double its present revenues and this economic system.

5

BALANCING
THE FIELD

The single most important factor for ensuring baseball's success in the future is for the sport to embrace a more comprehensive revenue-sharing plan. This isn't as much fun as talking about the playoff system, nor is it as interesting as the arguments over the DH. But it has to be Point One. Without it, nothing else is even worth the trouble. If baseball is serious about solving its problems—if the sport's caretakers want any concessions from players or any sign of support from fans—then this has to come first.

The solution can't just be a Robin Hood scheme that takes from the rich and gives to the poor. It needs to embody a new paradigm of cooperation that can guide the league through the next century.

And when you talk revenue sharing, you have to talk about local broadcasting revenues. As we've seen, this is the primary source of the automatic revenue inequity (as opposed to fluctuating revenue streams tied largely to performance, like ticket sales, concessions, and souvenirs).

Take a look at Table 1, which lists the broadcasting revenues for all 30 major league teams in '99. Many of these numbers are estimates, since Major League Baseball guards the actual figures as if they were the combination to Scrooge McDuck's bank vault. (In some cases, as with Atlanta, the Dodgers, and the Chicago Cubs, the estimates are not of the actual figures of the contract but of the *overall market value* of these contracts, since companies in these cases own both the teams and the networks on which its games are broadcast, making exact figures hard to come by, and deceptive when they are identified.)

You can tell quickly that there is a staggering difference in revenue. Even after factoring in the $15 million in national revenue that goes to each club because of the national TV contract (and MLB Properties), there's still a $55 million difference between what the richest team

TABLE 1.
BROADCASTING REVENUE (IN $ MILLIONS)

	Local	National	Total
NY Yankees	58	15	73
Chicago Cubs	56	15	71
Atlanta	51	15	66
NY Mets	39	15	54
Los Angeles	33	15	48
Baltimore	25	15	40
Arizona	24	15	39
Anaheim	23	15	38
Chicago White Sox	23	15	38
Boston	21	15	36
Cleveland	21	15	36
Colorado	19	15	34
Philadelphia	18	15	33
Detroit	17	15	32
San Francisco	17	15	32
Seattle	17	15	32
Toronto	17	15	32
Florida	15	15	30
Houston	15	15	30
St. Louis	15	15	30
Texas	15	15	30
Cincinnati	12	15	27
Oakland	12	15	27
Tampa Bay	12	15	27
San Diego	10	15	25
Milwaukee	9	15	24
Pittsburgh	7	15	22
Kansas City	6	15	21
Minnesota	5	15	20
Montreal	3	15	18

(the Yankees) and the poorest team (the Expos) make from broadcasting. Not coincidentally, this discrepancy accounts for much of the Yanks' $77 million payroll advantage over the Expos in '99.

Baseball's situation is particularly acute because more than half of its broadcast revenues come from local TV and radio rights fees. This is in stark contrast to the NFL, which receives some $70 million per year per team for its national broadcast rights, more than enough to cover each team's main expense, its player payroll, before a single ticket is sold. Since all NFL games are network telecasts, and since there are only 16 games in a season, local broadcast revenues are small and inconsequential.

But what's true of national telecasts is equally true of local telecasts: You don't have a game without two major league teams. The New York Yankees make $58 million a year in local broadcasting revenues, but the money comes because they're playing games against other major league teams. Yankee intrasquad games are not broadcast, and wouldn't be watched in such numbers if they were.

It's perfectly logical, then, to give half of each team's local money to its opponents. A more streamlined solution (one that also anticipates and compensates for any difference in schedules due to interleague play or unbalanced schedules) would allow each team to keep half of its own revenue while placing the other half in a national pool, which would then be divided equally among all 30 clubs. Presently, teams share equally in national revenue but keep all the local revenue themselves (save the revenue-sharing contribution some make). After this change, teams would share equally in all national revenue and share equally in *half* of all local revenue. It's a significant change, one with broad implications and real potential to address revenue inequity.

But notice that the principle is not mere charity. The Yankees and Dodgers get the same share from this pot as the A's and Pirates. Of course, they contribute more to it in raw dollars, but proportionally, their contribution is the same: one-half. Such a system would put about $300 million into the general pool, which would then be divided 30 ways, giving each team about $10 million.

This simple solution goes a long way toward solving the problem. As seen in Table 2, the range between the richest and poorest teams is sliced in half, down to $27 million from $55 million.

Now, when this book comes out, someone's going to complain that these numbers are inaccurate. I'll be the first to agree with them: The fact is, by the 2000 season, the actual total for both local and national TV and radio revenues will be *greater* than the numbers you see here. But identifying any hard set of numbers is like trying to jump on a speeding train. Rights fees, after the stunning deals garnered by the NFL and, most recently, the NCAA

TABLE 2.
BROADCASTING REVENUE (IN $ MILLIONS)

	Before	*After*
NY Yankees	73.0	54.3
Chicago Cubs	71.0	53.3
Atlanta	66.0	50.8
NY Mets	54.0	44.8
Los Angeles	48.0	41.8
Baltimore	40.0	37.8
Arizona	39.0	37.3
Anaheim	38.0	36.8
Chicago White Sox	38.0	36.8
Boston	36.0	35.8
Cleveland	36.0	35.8
Colorado	34.0	34.8
Philadelphia	33.0	34.3
Detroit	32.0	33.8
San Francisco	32.0	33.8
Seattle	32.0	33.8
Toronto	32.0	33.8
Florida	30.0	32.8
Houston	30.0	32.8
St. Louis	30.0	32.8
Texas	30.0	32.8
Cincinnati	27.0	31.3
Oakland	27.0	31.3
Tampa Bay	27.0	31.3
San Diego	25.0	30.3
Milwaukee	24.0	29.8
Pittsburgh	22.0	28.8
Kansas City	21.0	28.3
Minnesota	20.0	27.8
Montreal	18.0	26.8

basketball tournament, are going up throughout sports. And it has become clear, after ESPN and Major League Baseball settled their dueling lawsuits in December of '99, that the baseball numbers are heading in the same direction. So the one thing we know for sure is that the above numbers are a conservative estimate of the money on the table.

So for the purposes of explaining this plan, the actual numbers aren't important. If such a plan was put in place, there would surely have to be an outside audit to calculate the real value of each team's local contract. But that's what lawyers, auditors, and accountants are for. What matters here are the operating principles. All appropriately shared revenues (and that includes additional upcoming revenues, such as the Internet windfall that may be on the horizon) are plugged into this equation. The figures will change, but the concept—of sharing equally half of all local broadcasting revenues and all of the national broadcasting revenues—will hold.

Back to the plan: At this point, the big-market clubs are screaming bloody murder—and they'll still be screaming when this chapter comes to an end. But this is the only way to come anywhere close to getting a balanced playing field in baseball, and it should have been implemented long ago. It will hurt some clubs right now—the Yankees' profits would be sliced by almost $20 million per year—but overall, baseball will be better. And the Yankees and teams like them will still be profitable.

Wellington Mara, owner of the New York Giants, faced a similar situation, and made a similar decision, 40 years ago. At the time, Pete Rozelle, the new commissioner of the NFL, was pushing for a league-wide television contract that would replace all the existing local deals and pay Green Bay and Pittsburgh the same fees as the New York Giants and Chicago Bears. By agreeing to the we're-all-in-this-together principle, Mara not only guaranteed the survival of proud clubs like the Packers and Steelers, he helped his own cause in the long run— as the NFL made billions in the decades ahead.

Such is the situation facing the big-market clubs here. George Steinbrenner, Ted Turner, Rupert Murdoch, and the like have to understand that increasing revenue sharing is as crucial to them in the long run as it is to small-market owners in the short term. It will improve the overall product and the competitiveness of the game, and provide a stabilizing influence on all markets; it is an essential first step toward seeking some form of salary restraint from the players.

The 50/50 team/league split of local broadcasting revenues has the virtue of being connected to a rock-solid principle that doesn't have anything to do with altruism. Instead, it's based on a sound understanding of the cooperative nature of leagues.

This is the only way to equitably spread the wealth and help balance the playing field. Any other plan that I've seen either goes too far toward complete revenue sharing (reducing the incentive for teams that is crucial for this to work) or uses the ends to justify the means (arbitrarily robbing from the rich and giving to the poor, without recognizing that there is some room for fluctuation in the identities of "poor" and "rich" teams). Any mere tinkering with the present system only perpetuates the owners' myopic, too-little-too-late solution of '95, which continues to provide many middle- and lower-echelon teams with a disincentive to pay competitive salaries, hurting all of baseball in the process.

Now the cold, hard truth: This, in itself, is not enough. Baseball also needs to make an effort to share some ticket revenue as well. The AL once had an 80/20 split, but that was wiped out in the collective bargaining agreement of 1995. It was replaced by the ineffectual revenue-sharing and luxury tax, which took several million dollars from the top few teams and gave them to the bottom few. This is the equivalent of John D. Rockefeller offering a street urchin a shiny new dime. It doesn't hurt, it may even be much appreciated, but at the end of the day, it doesn't really change the position of either person.

It's also time to share some of the windfall that clubs like Baltimore, Cleveland, and Arizona have realized from their new ballparks. So part two of the proposal would call for revenue sharing in ticket sales as well. Home teams would keep 70 percent of their ticket revenues. The remaining 30 percent of each team's ticket sales (including tickets for luxury boxes) would then be divided equally among the 30 teams.

In the most extreme case, the Orioles figure to lose about $11 million from their $72 million gate, and a few other big franchises (especially those with new parks) might lose between $5 and $8 million at first. Remember that 30 percent is still less than the 60/40 Home/Road split employed by the NFL.

As you can see in Table 3, a 70/30 split helps narrow the ticket-revenue range from nearly $64 million to less than $45 million. This can only help to make more teams more competitive, and the fewer teams that enter a season with no chance whatsoever, the better off the league is. These changes wouldn't eliminate the revenue gap, but they'd give the smaller markets a fighting chance— those clubs would be back in the baseball business.

Of course, neither of these steps is a solution unto itself. But taken together, they give us a blueprint for revenue distribution that comes much closer to being reasonable than anything baseball has given us lately.

When you combine broadcast and ticket revenues, under the old system the Yankees' annual gross is more than $100 million greater than Montreal's. Under the

TABLE 3.
TICKET SALES REVENUE (IN $ MILLIONS)

	Old	New
Baltimore	72.8	61.1
NY Yankees	60.5	52.5
Cleveland	60.1	52.3
Colorado	60.1	52.3
Atlanta	59.8	52.0
St. Louis	49.4	44.8
Texas	48.3	44.0
Boston	47.8	43.6
Arizona	46.7	42.9
Toronto	40.2	38.3
Seattle	39.5	37.8
Tampa Bay	39.0	37.5
Chicago Cubs	37.8	36.6
Los Angeles	37.7	36.6
NY Mets	36.9	36.0
Anaheim	29.8	31.0
Houston	29.1	30.6
San Diego	29.0	30.5
San Francisco	22.1	25.7
Florida	21.3	25.1
Chicago White Sox	20.1	24.3
Philadelphia	19.3	23.7
Milwaukee	18.6	23.2
Kansas City	16.0	21.4
Cincinnati	15.0	20.7
Detroit	14.7	20.5
Pittsburgh	14.6	20.4
Oakland	13.0	19.3
Minnesota	9.6	16.9
Montreal	9.1	16.6

new plan, the Yankees–Expos range would be reduced by about 40 percent, to just over $60 million.

This is hardly a pure socialist's dreamscape, but it's a substantial improvement. And it would lead to some ancillary gains that might not be immediately apparent. Under such a system, every team would have an opportunity to be competitive.

Remember, the figures you see here represent the minimum benefit of this plan. But think of the ongoing impact: The attendance and accompanying revenues of the smaller-market teams will almost certainly rise, as each club now has both the means and the motivation to improve its roster. Just as significantly, when all aspects of the plan are in place, the general perception that baseball enjoys something much closer to true competitive fairness and roster stability will change the entire atmosphere of the game. Fans in smaller cities will again have reason to believe in their team's possibilities, and to express that belief at the ticket window. Plus (and this is a huge plus), in an atmosphere of increased stability, there will again be the prospect of long romances with a team's marquee stars, rather than the dispiriting short flings that rob the game of some of its charm and sense of connection.

The focus could thus shift back to a team's success on the field, while making financial success off the field possible. And a powerful carrot for both competitive and economic improvement would still exist. Teams would still be motivated to maximize their attendance, because they'd still be directly making 70 cents on every dollar of ticket sales. And since the nonticket stadium revenue (parking, concessions, souvenirs) would go completely to those teams, there would be an even more powerful incentive to be competitive and sell tickets.

This would stand in stark contrast to the disincentive to be competitive that has allowed teams like Minnesota and Florida to trot out glorified Triple A teams in the last few years and improve their bottom line in the dreary process. Since the field would be more level to begin with, there would be little excuse for (or public tolerance of) such a no-win strategy.

Again, the good that accrues to baseball through comprehensive revenue sharing is greater than the sum of its parts. The revenue-sharing plan ought to put those teams pursuing the model of public-private funding for new stadiums in a better position to say to their municipalities, "This investment makes sense." Such a claim would carry credibility, in contrast to the present situation, where cities often feel as though they're simply pouring money down the drain, giving public welfare to high-price junkies.

Although the political and emotional pressures existing in any given city may often result in taxpayers coming across with huge portions of the funding for new stadiums, these expenditures can no longer be logically justified until baseball's economics have been fundamentally reformed. Fans in Milwaukee or Detroit may be told that their new parks will change everything, but here's what will really happen: Those clubs will be able to spend, say, $50 million on salaries instead of $30 or $35 million, but the disparities that now exist will just be perpetuated at higher levels. Don Fehr may be happy to see the gap between the Yankees and Brewers at $90 million to $50 million, rather than $70 million to $30 million, but it does little to solve the problem for Brewers fans, who will then be faced with ticket-price increases, the home team's constant carping about producing "new revenue streams," and a team that is scarcely more likely to contend.

The absurdity of this constant tail-chasing is best seen in my hometown of St. Louis. There is a strong consensus that it is the best baseball town in America. The Cardinals routinely exceed 3 million in annual attendance. With the Mark McGwire mania of the past couple of years, their attendance has been higher still, and one can safely assume that their merchandising revenues have soared as well. In recent years Busch Stadium has been remodeled, with natural grass replacing turf, and various retro touches (like a hand-operated out-of-town scoreboard) making it more appealing than ever to the Cardinals' loyal fans.

Nobody contends that Busch Stadium is anything other than a great place to watch a baseball game. It is beautiful, accessible, and a place where you can almost hear the cash registers singing. In a sane world, it would be many years before any serious talk of replacing Busch Stadium was heard. With their rich history and present popularity, the Cardinals should represent the very model of a successful sports franchise. The mere suggestion of the club being at a competitive or economic disadvantage should be laughable. And yet that very talk is being heard today, and seriously, with the Cardinals' ownership publicly posturing for a new stadium.

As far as I can tell, the Cardinal owners are decent sorts who genuinely love baseball and appreciate their team's tradition. And in the Alice in Wonderland economics of today's game, they're telling the truth in a way. If circumstances remain essentially the same and salaries keep spiraling at their present rate, the Cardinals *will* need a new stadium to increase their revenues so as to remain within hailing distance of the big-market clubs. And as far as stadium-building proposals go, theirs is a relatively enlightened one. But the ultimate answer to all this is not to be found in running out and building another new stadium to keep up with the Turners and Murdochs of the world. It's that the time has come to change the economics of modern baseball. Unless and until that happens, all attempts to secure public financing of new baseball stadiums must be viewed with suspicion, if not contempt. In almost every instance, it's ultimately a case of throwing good money after bad. It's pretty clear that, absent comprehensive economic reform, increased revenue streams don't solve anything but only keep the vicious cycle spinning.

There comes a time, of course, when all franchises need a new stadium. They needed one in Seattle, because the Kingdome was a monstrosity. The Twins should be out of the Metrodome for the same reason. Baseball palace though it may have been, Tiger Stadium was crumbling. Someday even Fenway and Wrigley will become museum pieces. And here is what municipalities should say when that time comes: "If baseball has a workable financial model in place, we are not only willing to help, we are happy to do so. Because under those circumstances, the investment can make sense. But until that is the case, kindly get lost."

With the revenue-sharing plan described earlier in this chapter, baseball would take the *first* step toward achieving a credible economic model. The newfound stability afforded by comprehensive revenue sharing itself would change the tenor of the game and the way it's portrayed in the media. Now, this doesn't solve all of baseball's problems, but these two methods of revenue sharing go a long way toward bringing baseball closer to the true meritocracy that any sports league should be.

Additionally and crucially, they put the caretakers of the game into a much better position to take the next vital step: bargaining with the players' union for some kind of restraint on salaries.*

---

* For the record, under baseball's revenue-sharing plan of the past few years, substantial funds went from the top few teams to the bottom few. However, there are at least two crucial flaws in this approach. (1) Without requiring teams to come up to a minimum payroll level, you have clubs on the receiving end of revenue sharing using the dough to improve their bottom lines but not their rosters. (2) It is not based on a comprehensive principle that should logically apply to all teams in a league, regardless of how revenue fluctuates. It's just a short-term handout and clearly has done absolutely nothing to ease competitive inequities.

6

UNION MEN

The story goes like this: During the 1998 season, the defending world champion Florida Marlins, languishing in last place with a skeleton of their '97 squad, finally made another move, dealing Bobby Bonilla and Charles Johnson to the Los Angeles Dodgers. Florida's clubhouse had become a ghost town by this point, and Bonilla and Johnson had just been dealt to a big-market club with tradition and a gorgeous ballpark, and one that was desperately trying to stay in a playoff race.

So when Bonilla was informed that he'd been traded to the Dodgers, his first reaction was to ask reporters, "Is there a state income tax in California?"

Now, I don't want to rip Bobby Bonilla, but I think most fans might have preferred if he'd asked, "How many games out of first are they?"

Fans have grown alienated from players in recent years, but not, I think, for the reasons many players suspect. It's not the money so much as the mind-set.

I think the modern fan understands that the game generates billions in revenue, and that players as a group are entitled to the lion's share of that revenue. Certainly, most fans would prefer that the money go in Derek Jeter's pocket rather than George Steinbrenner's.

What fans are asking, in return for the interest and support that make these players millionaires, is for them to give an honest effort, conduct themselves civilly, and be team players. But what they see is often something quite different.

We understand that money is an important factor, as it is with most people. But in the crass and graceless new world order of these times, money often seems to be the *only* factor to many players. Look, everybody wants to make a good living. But when those who are already fabulously wealthy seem to believe that further increasing that wealth trumps all other considerations—including the basic health and appeal of the institution from which they derive those riches—*that's* what grates on the reasonable fan.

So while there is resentment for players, I think it's too often oversimplified as a bald disgust over the dollars earned. Virtually no one bats an eye over the astronomical purses of boxers or the lavish endorsement deals enjoyed by athletes from all sports. In these instances, athletes really *are* analogous to entertainers. But that analogy, so glibly and self-servingly offered by the Players Association, does not hold up in team sports, because team stars must make their living within the context of an ongoing and practically functioning league. When the salary structure of a league becomes unworkable (i.e., it threatens competitive balance and team continuity), that is rightly the concern of fans in a way that the riches earned by entertainers or individual sports stars like Tiger Woods, Pete Sampras, and Mike Tyson are not.

But the money itself? It has long ago stopped meaning much in the life of the everyday fan. Making more than a million dollars a year is, for 99 percent of the population, an abstract concept to begin with. It's not like fans were sitting around saying, "Well, Barry Bonds is worth $7 million—I can live with that. But this Kevin Brown making $14 million—why, that's *madness*. I can't watch the game anymore."

I'd go as far as to say that if you could somehow present a system in which you told sports fans that the *aver-*

age salary would be $10 million a year, with superstars making $50 million, but that (1) teams from all markets would have a reasonable chance to compete, (2) hometown favorites would have as good a chance to remain hometown favorites as they once did, (3) player personnel moves would primarily be made from the standpoint of baseball, rather than economic, judgments, and (4) the average guy who's a big baseball fan could still afford to attend eight to 10 games a year—if all that could happen even with the average salary at $10 million, fans would accept it, most of them gladly. They might think, "Lucky dogs," but they wouldn't really care.

But it can't work that way, so there's reason for concern. Knowledgeable fans shudder when they consider the Seattle situation. New ballpark, huge revenue streams, can't hold the team together. Or think of what might have been if Mark McGwire's prodigious power weren't coupled with some sense of perspective and proportion. Luckily for Cardinals fans, McGwire accepted an $11 million option for 2001. He also had to accept the behind-the-scenes disapproval of agents and Players Association types who decried the missed chance to reestablish the market. McGwire, after all, might have commanded $20 million a season. However, this would have left the Cardinals, their fans, and McGwire himself to contemplate these irreconcilable facts: The Cardinals could either say goodbye to the man who had authored some of the most memorable moments in their franchise's history, and who had been so embraced by their city that they all but renamed the Arch for him, or they could keep him and, by so doing, leave themselves in such a payroll bind that the Cardinals would be doomed to continue as a McGwire home-run sideshow, not a contending baseball team. Surveying this landscape, fans see only madness.

What thinking fans object to is this current state of affairs, in which salaries average $1.6 million a year but only a few teams can reasonably hope to contend. And even among the strongest teams, roster turnover can be so dizzying that you can't tell the pennant winners without a scorecard.

So, since we're not going to some superleague of eight megamarket teams (which the Players Association doesn't want either), we have to look toward a system that will make sense. The keys to creating such a system are for both the high-end owners *and* the high-end players to agree to something far removed from Milton Friedman's or Ayn Rand's concept of an unfettered free market.

I know what you're saying: That may be reasonable, but good luck getting the Players Association to even consider it. This is the strongest and most doctrinaire union in the country. They have been extraordinarily successful protecting and promoting their members' interests.

But that's just the point. Many aspects of the present system are no longer in the best interests of a majority of the players.

In 1999, the only teams making profits on a cash-

flow basis were a few clubs at the top of the salary scale—
and a few at the bottom. (And perhaps the Cardinals, in
the middle, with Mark McGwire, though they insist they
lost money as well.) The competitive inequities prompted
several teams to gut their payrolls, figuring that the middle market was a no-man's-land. Kansas City slashed
$12 million in payroll in one year; Cincinnati's payroll
dropped $23 million over two years. This salary roller-
coaster ride is both costly and jarring for the players, who
are moving from team to team and being dropped from
long-term contracts at a higher rate than ever before. At
the same time, the overwhelming majority of players are
consigned to teams that have no real shot at the pennant.

And you can sympathize with the discontent of *those*
players. Take someone like Rondell White, the talented,
all-heart outfielder for the Expos. When he came out of
the blue and demanded a trade in Montreal in '99, you
could at least understand his motivation. Here's a proud
athlete who's built his whole life around the pursuit of
excellence. But he's stuck with a team that is unable to
make a serious attempt at contention.

The time has long since come for the players to see
that they have a stake in correcting this. To recognize
that while salaries are important, you also play the game
to compete and achieve, and the greatest competition,
the greatest achievements, the greatest rewards that the
game has to offer are found in the legitimate pursuit of a
championship.

The system desperately needs some stability, some equilibrium. Revenue sharing must come first, but competitive integrity also rests on some form of upward limitation on player salaries. This is provided, of course, that the upward limitation would benefit the rank-and-file players in the same way that revenue sharing benefits the small- and medium-market franchises.

It's been too easy for too long for the players to reject all appeals to soften their stance. Any management pleas for meaningful reform have been greeted with the same old retort: "The owners have always said the sky is falling." There was merit to this: While many individual owners are honorable people, as a group their dealings with the players have been monumentally shortsighted, incompetent, and often dishonest. Thus, the owners lost credibility, because the economic reality did not match their rhetoric. Now, however, it does.

Meanwhile, what the Players Association still thinks of as principle—no upward limitation on salaries—has become, in truth, a myopic and outdated view of the way the game should operate, a view that clearly is no longer in the best interests of the institution or, ironically, a majority of the players themselves.

Yet it's easy to see why they've stuck with this line. Over the years, informed observers have consistently sided with the players, dating back to the days of Curt Flood. There was a time in the late '60s and '70s when supporting the Players Association was a cause that progressive sports fans took up because it transcended the sports world and was connected to threads of egalitarianism and antiestablishment ideals that appealed to most of a generation. These stances communicated a measure of sophistication, a view of the world that was broader and more compassionate than that of the portion of America who insisted on referring to Muhammad Ali as Cassius Clay, or claimed that the end of the reserve clause was the end of baseball. We knew better. The players were right, in ways both big and small.

So the players grew richer, as they should have, but their true cause was about a kind of justice, self-determination, and basic fairness. We have come to see that that basic fairness includes a slice of the pie that makes a huge percentage of the players millionaires and beyond. No problem with that. Here's the problem: We have devolved to the point where money is the *only* consideration of these union men, where all appeals to consider values beyond the crassest self-interest are viewed as naive at best and ridiculous at worst.

What today's Players Association is about is often so far removed from the essential principles that Curt Flood was fighting for that it is almost unrecognizable. It is greed and ego cloaking itself in a shroud of moral superiority.

Look, Marvin Miller should be in the Hall of Fame. His impact on the game was profound and beneficial. Picking up where Miller left off, Don Fehr and Gene Orza have been tough, capable, and honest. But we have now reached a point where even those of us who have consistently supported the Players Association can see what they apparently cannot or will not: Those who were once the revolutionaries and reformers now run the risk of playing the reactionaries.

Despite their respective track records, there's no law that says the Players Association is perpetually right and the owners perpetually wrong. Even DiMaggio's streak eventually came to an end.

The truly progressive stance in the year 2000 calls for the players to join the owners in reshaping the game's economics. Through some combination of persuasion and pressure, the Players Association needs to see that competitive balance should be viewed as an essential working condition, as much or more of a concern for their membership as chartered flights, pensions, and per diem. And that competitive balance cannot be achieved without the players' participation in both the sacrifices and rewards of a new baseball economy.

7

THE FLOOR-TO-CEILING CAP

With increased revenue sharing, the owners will have made a bold, visionary move to ensure the game's long-term success, set their own house in order, and will have created an environment in which the small-market franchises have a reasonable chance to compete. It would be a watershed moment in baseball history.

But it addresses only half of the problem.

The second part of the equation is also crucial. Reducing the revenue gap works only if you can also come up with some mechanism that puts a ceiling on individual and team salaries. Otherwise, the same vexing disparities will keep occurring at even higher, more dangerous dollar levels.

The purpose here goes beyond a *drag* on salaries, which is pretty much what owners hoped to accomplish during the ill-fated negotiations of '94–'95. The proper objective of a salary cap, as with revenue sharing, is to enhance competitive balance and stabilize the game's economics. What it does to salaries is an important but secondary concern.

With competitive balance and stabilization as the goal, it's clear that any payroll cap must also be accompanied by a payroll minimum, since many teams' payrolls are now at unacceptably low levels (and greater revenue sharing would eliminate any plausible excuse for keeping them that low).

Now here's the good news, as far as the players are concerned: A salary-cap plan that included both a reasonable ceiling and a reasonable floor would, as it turns out, significantly increase players' salaries overall. Which is fine, if it works. And, in this case, it will.

Let's go over the elements of this plan, on a point-by-point basis, before considering the cumulative impact:

• A major league team-payroll minimum equal to the per-team average of media revenues (both local and national), and a maximum equal to twice that figure. For purposes of illustration, let's assume that by the time this was under discussion, the formula would lead to a payroll minimum of $40 million and a maximum of $80 million.

With that single change, you will have done more to restore competitive balance than any of baseball's misguided moves of the past decade. In 1999, the New York Yankees had a payroll six and one-half times as high as Florida's, six times as high as those of Montreal and Minnesota, five times as high as Kansas City's, and four times as high as Pittsburgh's. But this ceiling/floor proposal would mean that every team in major league baseball would have a payroll of at least half of the highest-paid team. (In 1999, only 15 of the other 29 teams could make this claim.)

If revenue sharing as described in Chapter 5 is instituted, a dozen major league teams will be in a much better position to increase their payrolls.

The purpose of a salary-cap plan, then, would be to ensure that you standardize the range of team payrolls to allow for greater competition, while ensuring that each club can (in fact, must) at least attempt to field a competitive team.

Now, this would obviously curb salary escalation at the top of the scale. An $80 million cap would force some teams, like the Yankees, to cut their payrolls from 1999 levels. And if this was all it did, the players would be justified, based purely on self-interest, in opposing the plan.

But, because the plan would also force 11 teams below the salary minimum of $40 million to raise their payrolls to that level, there would be widespread payroll increases elsewhere in the majors. Some teams, like Philadelphia, would need small payroll boosts, but others—like the Expos, Marlins, and Twins—all would be required to spend in the neighborhood of an additional $20–25 million each on players to reach the minimum. The cumulative amount of the payroll increases required to get everyone up to $40 million is $160 million, meaning that the players, as a group, would be $147 million ahead of where they were in 1999.

Now, in the present circumstances, these smaller-market teams can plead that they can't afford to spend that much more money. But with the increased revenue sharing proposed earlier, these teams will realize dramatic revenue increases and be in a much better position to afford those salaries. Payroll minimums simply ensure that teams like the Brewers and Pirates will put that added revenue back into their teams, to enhance competitive balance.

In almost every case, the dollars needed to reach the minimum are matched or exceeded by revenue gained. There are only two teams for which this formula doesn't balance: the Marlins and White Sox. In both cases, the mandated payroll increases substantially exceed the gains from revenue sharing. But both franchises are in an anomalous situation where, for reasons of their own, owners strip-mined the team's talent and started over from the ground up. Unpopular but perhaps justifiable strategies in the present environment; neither necessary nor permitted once we've straightened things out.

With the added revenue sharing, Major League Baseball has a right to ask all teams to reach these minimums. And any team that can't afford to do so will have proved, almost by definition, that it doesn't have a workable financial model.

Preemptive rebuttal here. Just as soon as such a plan was proposed, people would rise up from all corners, dismissing it as unrealistic. But take note: There's not a single team in the NFL or NBA that has a payroll more than double that of its competitors. Payroll equity is a central tenet of a fair competitive structure.

But the plan would also include:

• A "superstar" salary cap, limiting any one player's annual salary to one-quarter of the minimum team payroll or, if you prefer, one-eighth of the maximum team payroll. This would leave even the less-prosperous clubs the ability to offer their signature player a salary equal to that of what the big-market teams could offer. Based on the plan outlined above, that would put the superstar salary cap at $10 million.

The concept is more important than the exact figure, but as a starting point, given the team payroll parameters we've outlined, this seems a sound figure.

The only players asked to sacrifice would be a handful of top-drawer superstars. What they sacrifice is the chance to make even more riches: They would be asked, in order to help restore the health of the institution that has set them up for life, to now somehow accept being only as wealthy as emperors rather than as wealthy as sultans.

There's a rational reason for asking them to agree to these limits. The superstar salary cap asks the best players to make an investment in the overall well-being of the game, and as we will soon see, the well-being of the entire Players Association.

For decades, a Players Association mantra has been "The guys before me sacrificed for us. Now we have to do the same." This is a rallying cry that has led superstars and benchwarmers alike to forgo salaries during strikes. Here is a chance for the players who can most afford it to make a meaningful sacrifice, one they will hardly feel, yet one that will help the game and their fellow players immeasurably.

Why is a superstar cap necessary? Because even with a team cap, without individual ceilings, teams would still tend to spend wildly on superstars, leaving the rest of the league's players closer to league minimums, thus further adding to the striking disparity in salaries.

But for every concession the players are asked to give, they'll get something greater in return. In this case, the cap on superstar salaries is accompanied by good news for the rank and file. Among the headlines:

• A 50 percent increase in the minimum salary level, which increases from $200,000 to $300,000 (or perhaps even more if the owners really want to appeal to the rank and file in the upcoming negotiations).

In light of the vast amount of money spent on player salaries, it's still surprising how low the major league minimum is, especially since, at any one time, the single largest salary grouping is the one at or near the minimum level. Thus, this change alone affects vastly more players than the limit at the other end of the spectrum.

• Arbitration would still exist for players in their first four years in the majors, but only within a graduated scale of minimums and maximums for a player's first four years of service.

First-year players would all make $300,000. Second-year players would earn a minimum of $350,000, a maximum of $1 million. A third-year player would earn a minimum of $400,000 and a maximum of $2 million. Upon entering his fourth season, a player would earn a minimum of $500,000 and a maximum of $3 million. The salary minimum for all veterans with at least three years of service would then be $500,000.

Arbitration would still work to fix inequities and bring unreasonable salary demands (or unreasonably stingy salary offers) into line. But because it would occur within a fixed spectrum, it would no longer have the effect of skewing the entire salary scale.

• In exchange for the graduated caps, free agency would arrive two years earlier, with players eligible after four years rather than six years of major league service. In the fifth and sixth years, however, it would be a restricted free agency in which the player's present team could retain him by matching any offer made for the next two years of his services. Beyond six years, a player would become an unrestricted free agent.

This rule, like the superstar salary cap, would serve to increase the possibility that superstar players would choose to stay with their original teams. There can be few things as frustrating as watching a player come up through your system, establish himself as a star with your team, then leave it simply because the club can't make a competitive offer for his services.

For the players, who presently get unrestricted free agency after six years, there would be two possible benefits. Superstars and potential superstars would be able to realize their top value two years earlier (if a player is offered the superstar maximum, his present team has to either match it for the next two years or let him go; either

way, the player is making the maximum). For role players—a fourth outfielder, a reliable utilityman—those who
are more valued elsewhere would have a chance to find
their ideal fit two years earlier, with clubs willing to pay
them (or play them) more than their original team.

The rule here would serve to increase a player's freedom, because he can entertain outside offers two years
earlier and because, in the case of superstars, more teams
would now be realistically in the hunt for his services. So
while this would present the player with greater flexibility,
it simultaneously increases the likelihood that, all else
being equal, he'd wind up staying with his present club.

To close a potential loophole, it seems reasonable to
limit free-agent contracts to five years, with the provision
that a player could sign a longer deal with his present
team. In any case, all guaranteed contracts must count in
full against the cap.

It would seem fair that the owners guarantee the
players a substantial percentage of the game's defined
gross revenues. If somehow total salaries paid under the
floor-to-ceiling system didn't meet or exceed that figure,
the shortfall would be made up by the management to
the Players Association, for distribution as they saw fit.
The point as always is to restore competitive equilibrium,
not to unfairly suppress player compensation.

Let's take a look at the upshot of these five changes:

Competitive balance would be improved, because no team would have a payroll more than double that of any other team, a huge improvement over the present penthouse/outhouse model of payroll distribution.

Players would be better off, because they would collectively earn in the neighborhood of an extra $150 million per season, just for starters. That much is guaranteed, but it almost certainly understates the players' gains. The real-world result of this plan would likely find a number of clubs at all payroll levels willing to spend extra dollars given their now-more-realistic hopes of contending for a division title.

In the present system, it doesn't make competitive sense for the Blue Jays to increase their payroll from $48 million to $50 million, if the Yankees can simply respond by upping their payroll by twice as much. But with a cap, a competitive benefit to greater spending becomes more realistic, and the additional expense more justifiable, when the highest-spending teams can't turn around and reestablish their economic superiority.

Further, since the payroll minimums are tied to league TV revenues, payroll minimums would rise when the revenues increased. And the prospect of a sport with its house in order (to say nothing of a more stable environment and a better overall sense of structure and purpose to the game) would virtually guarantee an increase in the size of the pie in future years. So if the average team's broadcasting revenue rose to $48 million in the next deal, then the new minimum would be $48 million, the new maximum would be $96 million, and the new superstar maximum would increase proportionately, to $12 million, etc. Owners ought to be glad to pay these higher fares, because they'd come in the context of the entire game growing and being more profitable.

Again, all of these figures are subject to change. What matters is the framework. The updated figures can always be plugged in.

Owners would have what they've always needed: a spending ceiling that they couldn't exceed, that would serve to protect them from each other—and that would promote the game's competitive balance. There would still be losing teams, and probably some awful ones. But they'd be that way for all the time-honored baseball reasons of bad trades, bad farm systems, and bad luck, rather than built-in structural disadvantages.

Even small-market teams would again be able to build for the long term, through a prudent use of resources. Which brings up a fair question here: What if you're in the first or second year of a five-year plan, building a team around a nucleus of young players? You don't want to overpay them just to reach the minimum, but you expect this to be the heart of your team for the next decade. No problem: There would be a provision allowing any team to put money into a "payroll escrow" account, with the stipulation that if you come in $5 million under the cap in 2001, you will use that $5 million to go beyond the minimum sometime within the next five years. You'd still be forced to average at least the minimum over any five-year period, and if you didn't do so, the money would be turned over to the Players Association.

In any case, a resourceful team, at whatever payroll level, could devise its own approach to assembling a competitive roster without worrying that dramatic year-to-year market shifts would render their plan unworkable.

Fans would be much better served because they would see a better, fairer, more competitive product that would still be fluid enough for teams to build contenders, but that would have more continuity than the game did in the '90s. Superstars would be less likely to leave their teams for strictly monetary reasons. And yet they'd still be lavishly rewarded, making annual wages that would often exceed the operating profits of the teams for which they played.

Who would pay the price for all these changes? Those who can most afford it—and who will still thrive in the new system.

In absolute terms, the superstars of the game would be asked to live with less than they could make in an open market. But one would hope that the players would be able to realize, as their counterpart superstars in the NBA eventually did, that this sacrifice was serving the greater good of all the players, as well as the game itself.

And even the players who sacrificed most would be giving up far less than the other major contributor—the big-market clubs. Those clubs would accept decreases in both absolute revenue and inherent competitive advantages. They'd still have plenty of both, but not enough to give them a prohibitive edge.

Such a system could work. But to make it work, you have to implement both sides of the plan—greater revenue sharing and the floor-to-ceiling cap.

Taken together, these changes would eliminate the excuses by the small-market teams and the overwhelming advantages enjoyed by the big-market teams.

More teams with a perceived shot at being competitive when the season starts means greater overall ticket sales, greater broadcasting revenue, and a clearer appreciation for which club really has the best organization.

This last element is important. Normalizing the finances would ensure that the key to success would no longer be purely money. A team with an excellent farm system (like the Expos) would be rewarded for it. A team with a mediocre farm system (like, say, the Orioles) would be punished, unable to throw unlimited money after high-priced talent to extricate themselves from their rut (or, if even this is done poorly, dig themselves in deeper).

The focus, for the savvy baseball fan, would again be on the baseball virtues of personnel judgments and the horse-trading acumen of their team's GM. Fans could go back to viewing the game primarily as a game, rather than as a business that has taken over the game. They could do this at the same time that the business itself became more stable for the owners and more lucrative for the players as a group.

Thus, baseball's caretakers would have instituted the most radical change imaginable—one in which everybody wins off the field, and everyone begins with a chance on it.

8

IF IT AIN'T BROKE . . .
(THE FOOLISHNESS
OF RADICAL
REALIGNMENT)

Baseball is reliant upon its history to a far greater extent than any other sport.

If that doesn't seem self-evident, then consider this: Even avid football fans likely don't know what Walter Payton's career rushing record is, and have no idea what Jim Brown's total was before Payton got there. A much smaller percentage of fans know how many yards Edgerrin James rushed for in 1999 than know the statistics of a dozen different baseball players.

Dan Marino threw 48 touchdown passes in a season. Now, that's a great feat, but can you imagine the impact that a comparable performance would have in baseball? (If you watched baseball in 1998, you don't have to imagine.) If the nation buzzed with debate over the comparative merits of Marino and the previous record holders, Y. A. Tittle and George Blanda, I missed it.

Yet Mark McGwire and Sammy Sosa are forever linked with Babe Ruth and Roger Maris. Cal Ripken Jr. is forever linked with Lou Gehrig. Ken Griffey Jr. may be forever linked with Hank Aaron. This is unique to baseball, the only sport whose present and future are so dependent upon an understanding and appreciation of its past.

Given this, it continually surprises me that the caretakers of baseball still don't seem to have a clear sense of what the sport's strengths and weaknesses are, don't appear to grasp some of the game's most essential elements.

This has led to a sort of schizophrenia regarding baseball tradition. McGwire's home-run exploits are given their meaning by baseball's long history; old-style ballparks are all the rage; the Hall of Fame in Cooperstown and the Negro Leagues Museum in Kansas City draw large, enthusiastic crowds; Ted Williams and other greats grace the diamond at Fenway's All-Star Game, and it creates a moment unique to baseball. It should be obvious that much of the sport's appeal is retro, that a certain timelessness and connection to history are an enduring and indispensable strength.

And yet there's a sense that baseball is out of step, that it's losing touch with the country, and that it must continually provide novelty so as to somehow increase its hipness quotient. Part of this impulse comes from a sense of squeamishness (which I share) about wallowing in endless nostalgia. But part of it is sheer panic, a sign of leaders running to catch the prevailing winds of the cultural zeitgeist.

And nowhere is this sense of panic more pronounced—or less justified—than in the bizarre discussion about "radical realignment," which reached a fever pitch shortly after the beginning of interleague play in 1997. Out of nowhere, baseball people—led by Commissioner Bud Selig—were talking about wholesale movement of teams among divisions and leagues for the sole purpose of grouping as tightly as possible according to geography, all other considerations be damned.

What seems to be lost on them is this: There is an either/or distinction between interleague play and radical realignment. If the first is appealing, and you wish to maintain that which makes it so, then you can't even consider the second. And yet the commissioner of baseball has come out in favor of radically reconfiguring baseball's leagues and divisions along purely geographic boundaries. The concept continues to be discussed and, in some quarters, advocated. Therefore, it must be addressed, though the whole thing is absurd on its face.

Let me ask this: Who decided that the historic rivalry between the National League and American League was somehow bad for baseball? At a time when baseball needs to play to its strengths—and when the appeal of distinct leagues is the very reason why limited interleague play has any merit at all—some baseball people have reached a conclusion that is diametrically opposed to the evidence at hand. They think the sport would be better without these unique differences.

And the monumental, towering reason most frequently cited for such convulsive change? Starting times for away games. The thought process of realignment proponents goes like this: If all the Pacific time zone teams (AL and NL combined) were in the same division, midwestern and eastern teams would have fewer late starts at the Pacific parks.

Not having your favorite teams' games start at odd hours is a legitimate, if marginal, concern. (Ironically, this concern was cited to block the first move toward realignment, Fay Vincent's sensible and politically fatal decision to move the Cardinals and Cubs to the NL West, the Braves and Reds to the NL East, in 1992.) But in the big picture, it's clear that a handful of late starts for away games, or the occasional extra hour aboard a plane, pales in importance alongside the way the two leagues are embedded—as distinct and separate entities—in the American sporting consciousness.

And that's just for starters. There are other problems with realigning baseball along purely geographical lines. First, what really fuel rivalries are unbalanced schedules that emphasize divisional races. Teams don't have to change leagues or even divisions to accomplish that.

Even under the present balanced schedule, there's no real proof that geographic proximity guarantees rivalries. Instead, the evidence suggests that, as always, rivalries have more to do with competitive history than anything else.

The reason the Giants and Dodgers have a rivalry is, first, that they occupied the same *city* (not just time zone) for decades. Then, when they moved west in 1958, they were the only two western teams for a long time. And, crucially, they were contenders almost every year. If one or the other of them just flat-out stunk, the idea that the Giants and Dodgers would have carried with it the meaning that it had in New York, or that the rivalry would have been sustained solely by virtue of occupying the same state— even though they'd be hundreds of miles away—is ridiculous.

By the same token, look back to when the Braves

were in Boston and the Giants were still in the Polo Grounds. You had New York–Boston in the NL, just as you had New York–Boston in the AL. Yet the Braves–Giants series never had anything approaching the same sense of rivalry and mutual antipathy as Red Sox–Yankees, simply because the NL foes never developed the competitive history that animated the Red Sox–Yankees matchups.

And so it is when considering the present and recent past. New York and Kansas City are separated by 1,200 miles, yet in the '70s and '80s, the Yankees–Royals series was one of baseball's best and most heated rivalries. At roughly the same time, the Reds and Pirates had a thing of their own going. Cincinnati and Pittsburgh are geographically proximate, and these days they are in the same division. But like the Yankees and distant Royals, the rivalry is less fierce these days, simply because there's no competitive stake.

Over the last half-century, the distance between New York and Cleveland has gone unchanged. Yet in the '40s and '50s the rivalry between the Indians of Feller and Doby and the Yankees of DiMaggio and Mantle raged. Then, for more than 30 years, it was dormant. Why? Because the Indians were unceasingly awful. Now the Indians are a contender again, and the Yanks–Tribe matchups are brimming with excitement, in a way that Indians–Tigers (Great Lakes neighbors) does not now, and never has in my lifetime.

It seems crazy to distort the entire structure of the sport, throw out a century of history and context, and diminish or destroy existing rivalries, just so the tiny number of teams that would truly benefit from a gerrymandered regional arrangement could be accommodated. The benefit is so outweighed by the negative consequences that you wonder how the matter even got to the discussion stage.

Has baseball really given enough thought to what comes with mangling the leagues for the sake of a few attractive matchups? It means a New York baseball fan gets the Phillies and Blue Jays twice as often, the Dodgers and Mariners once in a blue moon. That's progress? Only in the through-the-looking-glass world of those who rave about interleague play, propose to blow up the leagues, and then, with a straight face, would label a Pirates–Giants contest an "interleague" game.

Baseball's present structure, even beyond the history of the AL and the NL, is to its advantage. It is not a coincidence that the two most popular professional sports in America, football and baseball, each have two coast-to-coast league structures under a larger league umbrella, rather than a purely regional league separated into geographic conferences, as the NBA and NHL have.

Just as the AL was originally a competitor to the NL, the AFL was originally a competitor to the NFL. In both cases, the upstart league proved its mettle, established an identity, and then deepened that sense of identity long after a truce with the elder league.

Long after the NFL–AFL merger, the idea of each conference having a personality, and even to some extent its own fan base, still holds. Same for baseball, with the NL and the AL. But no such enduring identities exist in hockey or basketball. Oh, sure, there are years where someone observes that the more physical basketball teams are in the East, or that that the better goalies are in the West, but these are simply incidental trends, not intrinsically tied to the identity of each group.

In football and baseball, those differences between leagues are pronounced (and one of the by-products of the designated hitter rule, it must be granted, is to under-score the differences between a style of play in the NL and a style of play in the AL). And so, even in an age of interleague play in both sports, there is still league pride in baseball and conference loyalty in football.

Radical realignment would transport baseball to the basketball-hockey model, which is less complex, less resonant, and less truly national. And in place of the three-quarters-of-a-century AL vs. NL rivalry in the Mid-summer Classic, it would give us a de facto East–West All-Star Game. Please, hold your applause.

Unlike the addled concept of radical realignment, for which no convincing arguments can be advanced, there is a case to be made that some limited interleague play enhances the game, increases fan interest and attendance, and can do so without significantly damaging the essential fairness of baseball's regular season. But that which is appealing about the idea of interleague play—the opportunity for crosstown rivals to tangle (Yankees–Mets, Cubs–White Sox), as well as the novelty of Boston visiting San Diego or Seattle taking a road trip to Wrigley Field—is rooted in the historical and ongoing *distinction* between the National League and American League.

Remember, too, the justification used for Milwaukee's move from the AL to the NL in 1998. When baseball wanted an AL team to switch leagues (so that both leagues would continue to have an even number of teams), the Brewers went largely because Milwaukee viewed iteslf, historically, as a National League city—its only World Series flag was flown by an NL representative.

To the extent that the history of a sport has significance in the present, it comes through continuity. That continuity shouldn't be violated on a mere whim. There are certain extraordinary times when making major changes to a long-standing league structure becomes necessary (as when the NL and AL split into two divisions in 1969, or when the 16-team NFL and 10-team AFL merged, prompting the move of Cleveland, Baltimore, and Pittsburgh from the old league to the new). But only if there's some greater reason for it. No such reason exists in baseball today.

The key to mapping baseball's future is to preserve that which is valuable, important, and relevant about the game's historical continuity and structure, while modifying the areas where the game needs to be updated. Limited interleague play, properly formatted, meets that standard. Radical realignment falls short of even the minimum standards of common sense.

9

RADICALLY SIMPLE
REALIGNMENT

If we've established that radical realignment isn't the way to go, it's also clear that *some* change is required. We know that we want to move to an unbalanced schedule, in which division rivals play more games against each other. But trying to implement an unbalanced schedule and conduct interleague play in a setup with 16 teams in one league and 14 in the other is a scheduling nightmare.

It has been suggested, with some logic, that baseball would be well-advised to buy out at least two of its weakest sisters and get back to 28 teams. The purpose would be threefold: (1) two fewer teams to worry about in revenue sharing, (2) a larger cut of all shared revenues, especially network TV, for the remaining teams, and (3) a less diluted talent pool. This makes sense, but 28 teams leaves baseball with fewer workable options regarding scheduling and divisional setups than does 30. Going the other way, and expanding to 32, balances divisions, but four four-team divisions, with their mini-champion, in each league, is a joke. Almost as big a joke as the idea that fifty more big leaguers will fall out of the sky on the day of the expansion draft.

The truth is, in a perfect world, baseball would have 24 teams, aligned in two six-team divisions per league. The baseball would be better, and the pennant races would make more sense, but there is no practical way to make six teams disappear, and removing two or even four doesn't work in terms of divisional alignments or scheduling, especially if we wish to include interleague play.

The other problem with contraction is this: More than 24 franchises have a fan base that has proved it will support baseball if some semblance of a competitive team is placed on the field. You can make a case for cutting Montreal based on a longtime lack of fan support. You can even cut Tampa Bay, citing a marked drop in attendance in only its second season. You might even argue for cutting Oakland, based on the idea that two teams can't fly in the Bay Area market. But that brings you down to 27 franchises, a no-man's-land. Some would say the next three franchises on the cutting block could be Pittsburgh—which played in the very first World Series, has a significant and glorious history, and has a new stadium on the way—and Minnesota and Kansas City, two world championship–winning franchises that have shown, even in the past decade, they have a rabid fan base that will turn out in numbers easily exceeding 2 million, provided they have anything like a decent club to root for. Lopping off these franchises to pay for baseball's mismanagement amounts to blaming the victim.

So, for the purpose of this argument, let's assume that major league baseball will stick with 30 teams for the foreseeable future, and that they will remain in the cities or at least the time zones where they are now. In a 30-team universe, the more logical setup is a 15–15 breakdown.

But that alignment, if you'll recall, was rejected out of hand by major league baseball prior to the 1998 season, when it expanded to 30 teams. It was unthinkable, the sport's leaders said, because with a 15–15 setup, you'd be forced to play at least one interleague game on every day of the season that all 30 teams were in action.

But this objection raises the question: So?

At least one interleague game every day of the season

is admittedly not ideal, but neither is it a catastrophe. And with 30 teams and interleague play, it's the only reasonable way to go. The notion that these games have to be played in blocks—like some Mardi Gras of Interleague Play—is nonsense. If you're watching the Red Sox facing the Cardinals, what do you care whether the Indians are playing the Phillies at the same time?

The schedule could be adjusted so that the teams playing interleague games at the very beginning of the season *and* down the stretch would be the fourth- and fifth-place teams in each division from the previous season, thus lessening the chance that contenders would be playing outside their league down the stretch.

And once you agree on that, then your formula is clear: You have three divisions in each league, five teams in each division.

And here is each team's schedule:

Within the division:

   4 opponents x 18 games = **72 games**

     (6 home-and-away 3-game series with each opponent)

Within the league, outside the division:

   10 opponents x 6 games = **60 games**

     (2 home-and-away 3-game series with each opponent)

Interleague:

   5 opponents x 6 games = **30 games**

     (2 home-and-away 3-game series with each opponent)

                162 games

Now one stipulation has to be placed on this formula. The interleague play, for the sake of (1) the integrity of the divisional races, and (2) allowing each city to eventually see stars from the other league, must cycle around among the three divisions (rather than remain fixed on a West vs. West, Central vs. Central, East vs. East format as it has been since 1997).

If in 2001 the breakdown is East vs. East, Central vs. Central, and West vs. West, then a year later it ought to be East vs. Central, Central vs. West, and West vs. East, and then the following year East vs. West, Central vs. East, and West vs. Central.

Not only would this guarantee that every team would come to every park once every three years, but it would have the advantage of being, over any three-year period, an equitable and fair apportionment of opponents.

True, the Mets and Yankees and Cubs and White Sox would play only once every three years. But those series would then be truly special again. They already feel less special now that they're playing a bunch of games on an annual basis. Meanwhile, what should have been obvious at the beginning of all the interleague ballyhoo has now dawned on just about everyone: The Yankees and Derek Jeter ain't coming to Cincinnati. And, under the present shortsighted system, they never will.

Apart from the obvious intracity matchups, almost all interleague games have already become humdrum. With a rotation system, the novelty is maintained for all interleague opponents, and the once-every-three-year visits of superstars or marquee teams are truly special gate-boosting events.

Another benefit that springs to mind: With the above formula, all series during the season (save the makeup doubleheaders created by postponements) can become three-game series. This makes travel much easier for the players, and eliminates the spate of two-game series that they complained about in the early interleague scheduling. Also, by junking the balanced schedule, we've returned to the tried-and-true principle of scheduling more games against divisional opponents, for the purpose of both competitive integrity and September drama.

So if you conclude that 15–15 makes more sense than 16–14 (or, God help us, further expansion to 16–16), the question to ask then is: Who moves?

If you're at 16 and 14, there's no point even thinking about moving an AL team to the NL, because that then increases the number of teams that have to be moved back the other way.

So it needs to be an NL team moving to the AL, ideally into the now-four-team American League West, so that no further realignment is needed within the AL.

Milwaukee went over to the NL willingly and clearly doesn't want to go back. There's no point in sending a

team from the NL East, because that would require further shifting within the AL's divisions. The NL West quin-
tet of Arizona, Colorado, San Francisco, San Diego, and
Los Angeles makes sense and shouldn't be tampered with.

So that brings us back to the NL Central, where the
Cubs, Reds, Pirates, and Cardinals are part of the National
League's lore, and where the Brewers seem well placed.

And so, really, there is only one team that can and
should move: the Houston Astros.

They would go from the National League Central to
the American League West. They pick up a heated natural
rival just up the highway in the Texas Rangers. And, just
like that, baseball has two 15-team leagues, each with
three five-team divisions.

An objection to this would be the one posed earlier,
about Central time zone teams being forced to play more
games in the Pacific time zone, supposedly resulting in lost
revenue because of smaller TV audiences watching the
games. But guess what? Houston, playing the NL's balanced schedule, plays 30 games in the Mountain or Pacific
time zones already (six each at San Diego, San Francisco,
Los Angeles, Arizona, and Colorado). In the AL, with the
unbalanced schedule described above, they'd play only 27
games in the Pacific time zone and none in the Mountain.
They actually come out ahead on start times.

And Houston, in addition to experiencing a negligible
effect on road games, would pick up their rivalry with the
Rangers.

Now, the Astros have been in the NL for 38 years, and they pride themselves on their position. Still, they have never represented the Senior Circuit in the World Series, and their National League connection does not run so deep as to render a move unthinkable. With a guarantee of a regular rivalry with the Rangers, and perhaps some financial considerations for their cooperation, it seems reasonable that they could be convinced to move.

The added benefit is that Texas, which has agitated for moving out of the AL West, would now have a greater reason to stay there, the 18 games per season with the Astros more than compensating them for any perceived drawback to a schedule that includes a few more West Coast start times.

Baseball's supposed realignment crisis is solved—not with radical realignment, but with one single franchise shifting leagues, leaving the NL and AL with three five-team divisions. All factors considered, this is the simplest, cleanest, and most logical move.

But you might be asking yourself right now: If we stay with the three-division format, doesn't that mean you're committed to sticking with the wild card?

I thought you might bring that up. . . .

10

PENNANT RACES AND WILD CARDS

For a week last October, the New York Mets and Atlanta Braves staged one of those memorable playoff series that serve as a showcase of the sport at its best. In the National League Championship Series, Atlanta took the first three games, by a total of four runs. But the Mets, who had been chasing the Braves all year long, wouldn't be swept aside, and came back behind John Olerud's terrific performance in Game 4. Then came the dramatic bottom-of-the-15th rally, which was capped by Robin Ventura's "grand slam single," to win Game 5. By the time the Braves returned to face the Mets, in a tense, well-played Game 6 back in Atlanta, all the seats were finally filled at Turner Field, and Braves fans spent most of the game on the edge of them, before the spunky, battling Mets were dispatched.

Great series, great baseball, great moments.

And there are people who think that the simple fact that the Mets, a wild-card team, made such a dazzling show of the NLCS somehow justifies the wild card, proves the point that it's good for the game. But this small-sample lapse of logic is all wrong, a bit like saying that your four-pack-a-day uncle Louie, who lived to be 90, proves that cigarette smoking isn't harmful.

On this issue, baseball has been wrong. But in 1999, it was also very lucky.

Those NLCS games were great games, about as gripping as baseball gets. But the fact remains that the two teams should have showed that intensity a few weeks earlier, when they found themselves separated by a single game at the beginning of a stretch in which they'd play each other six times in nine days. Without the safety net of the wild card, those regular-season games between the Mets and Braves would have felt completely different. Truly compelling. No amnesty, no second chances, just the opportunity to prove who's got the best team at the end of the regular season's long road.

But because of the wild card, those six regular-season games—of which the Braves won five, continuing their season-long mastery of the Mets—didn't have anywhere near the urgency they should have. Going in, both teams knew there was little at stake. Only a complete collapse would cost either team a playoff spot.

Of course, it wound up being interesting at the end of the season, because the Mets provided just such a collapse, losing seven straight games at one point, before righting themselves on the final weekend of the regular season.

And so the last few days of the regular season proved exciting, but for all the wrong reasons. The Mets *slumped* their way back into a wild-card race, and in so doing muddied the clarity of the Houston–Cincinnati race in the Central. Without the wild card, either race might have had a win-or-else drama, and the conclusiveness of the result that comes with it. Instead, everything felt tentative and contingent. Less a pennant race than a game of musical chairs, with the regular season eliminating just one of the four participants.

Even here, baseball nearly came face-to-face with a travesty of its own making. The Mets and Reds finished tied for the wild card. But had Houston lost just one more game, or had the Mets and Reds each won one more, there then would have been two ties—a two-way tie for the NL Central title, and a three-way tie for the wild card. Then, instead of reveling in the few days of fluke excitement the system provided, everyone would have been bemoaning its idiocies and inequities. The Reds and Astros would have played one game for the Central title, while the Mets would have received an automatic pass into the playoffs through no logic or achievement (simply by having a one-half-game edge over the playoff game's loser). Out of dozens of possibilities, almost all of them working against the basic excitement and justice of pennant races, 1999's last week fell into a narrow slot in which the wild card's absurdities were camouflaged and, for a few days, drama and excitement ensued. Look, I enjoyed it, too—but enjoying it isn't the same as being blind to the system's larger flaws.

Here are some hard truths you can't get past: Pennant races are the lifeblood of baseball's history. Wild cards are the product of modern times. And in baseball, you have to choose one or the other. You can't have them both. The two things are mutually exclusive. It is that understanding, that simple regard for common sense, rather than an excessive regard for tradition, that accounts for my opposition to it.

The supposed advantages of the three-division-and-wild-card format are that it creates another round of playoffs and gives more teams the hope of having a shot at the postseason. As last season proved, it does these things, but at a prohibitive price.

It would be one thing if these features could be added to what already existed. But in fact they are created at the expense of everything that was legitimate and truly dramatic about baseball's regular season and authentic pennant races.

Enough time has passed that the new system can be judged on its merits. It's worth taking a detailed look back at what has been lost and what has been gained in the transition to the three-division format and the wild card.

Since even the gains are suspect at best, and illusory at worst, let's start with the substantial losses, the price we've paid for this particular dose of progress.

First, a point so obvious that no one in or around baseball should have to be reminded of it: A pennant race is not the same thing as the mere act of qualifying for the playoffs. A pennant race has specific competitive and dramatic characteristics. A pennant race possesses a certain remorseless justice—a kind of unforgiving insistence on excellence—that is unique and central to its appeal. All of those characteristics are destroyed or diminished by the wild-card system.

Under the existing system, it is impossible to have a meaningful race for first place involving the two best teams in the league (or any of the three best, for that matter). Not unlikely—*impossible*—since, by definition, any quality team that did not finish first in such a scenario would be the wild card. And if by chance the three best teams in the league were all in one division, then the meaningful race would be for second place, not first, since only the third-place finisher would be eliminated.

Let's suppose that two teams, each bound for a hundred wins, are in the same division. At the All-Star break, they are pulling away from the league but are neck-and-neck with each other. How can this possibly be a pennant race? Whoever is second is the wild card. There is no urgency. No tension. No drama.

And it's not just the best races that are robbed of meaning—the competition in every division is reduced in intensity. A race between two mediocre teams in a weak division can't really heat up, because the hotter the teams get, the more likely it is that they'll move into the wild-card picture, and so an element of the relentless pressure and desperation that so often characterize September baseball is inevitably diminished.

Even if it turns out that a division champion winds up with a worse record than the wild-card team, the possibility of wild-card amnesty deadens the tension that used to build over the course of a season. What made the Atlanta–San Francisco race so compelling in 1993 was the severity of the justice: From the moment the Braves began their late-summer rally, they knew that they couldn't afford to let up, because anything short of catching the Giants wouldn't be good enough.

That was perhaps the last great pennant race we'll ever see (the purists will insist we call it a divisional race, but those races felt like pennant races in a way that noth-

ing since '93 has). Imagine how anticlimactic Giants–
Braves would have been if the wild card had been in
place.

Actually, you don't have to, since every season since
then has produced ample evidence of how gimmicky the
wild card is, and how damaging it is to the entire idea of
pennant races. Yet baseball, and many of those who cover
it, continue to proclaim it a success. In truth, it should
have been obvious before they ever played a game under
this system that the combination of the wild card, mini-
divisions, and the balanced schedule would produce one
absurdity after another.

And it has. Let's go back:

1998: There are times when I wonder if logic and
facts play any part in all of this. That's how I felt through
much of the summer of '98, when I heard not fans but
writers and broadcasters opine, "Thank goodness for the
wild card, because without it, there'd be only one good
race out of six." How quickly they forget. Under its
present format, baseball has six divisions *because* of the
wild card and expanded playoffs. If baseball still had four
divisions, as it did in '93, then three of the four division
races in '98 would have been torrid, and the reason the
fourth would not have been was that in the New York
Yankees, the AL East featured one of the great single-
season teams of all time.

Not only would these races have been close, they
would have been infinitely more meaningful than the

tepid wild-card races that replaced them, since the winners would have been one step removed from the World Series instead of two. Does anyone really expect baseball fans to be talking years from now about memorable wild-card races? Does anyone remember which teams just missed the wild card even two or three years ago? And yet great pennant and divisional races resonate for decades, engaging not just the fans of those particular teams but baseball fans as a whole, adding to the game's lore.

1997: At the All-Star break, the Yankees trailed the Orioles by seven games. However, they led the wild-card race by four and a half. Yet the second half dawned with much speculation about whether the Yankees would catch the Orioles, as though that mattered in the least. We were told to circle our calendars for the dates of remaining "crucial" Yankees–Oriole games. In truth, the Yankees' remaining games with Chicago and Anaheim loomed larger, because those were the teams New York would have to hold off for the wild card, the only outcome of real consequence.

Yet the media remained fixated on a race for first when in fact what was really happening was more analogous to preliminary heats at a track meet: who is just above and just below the cutoff for the finals is all that really matters, and the difference between winning and finishing second is largely irrelevant.

This was also the year, of course, that a wild-card team won the World Series. In the National League, the

Florida Marlins qualified for the playoffs despite finishing nine games out in the NL East. They then beat San Francisco and edged Atlanta, emerging in the Series against the Cleveland Indians (who sported the fourth-best record in the American League that year).

While an extra-inning seventh game partially redeemed the World Series, through the first six contests it had nothing like the feel of a fall classic. Why? The matchup didn't compel because it seemed as much arbitrary as earned; it was the back end of a contrived and bloated October tournament rather than the final act of a season-long drama in which only the highest achievers remain onstage at the end.

The point here is that true baseball theater is driven by unique dynamics. What you can get away with in other sports doesn't necessarily work in baseball. No one remembers or much cares who finished first in the regular season in basketball or hockey—their regular seasons have always been viewed as little more than a prelude to the playoffs. But baseball's regular-season titles have always been viewed as distinct and important unto themselves. Of course, every team hoped to win the World Series, but winning the division or pennant was viewed as a major achievement.

Additionally, baseball doesn't offer slam-bam, moment-to-moment action. It isn't easily enhanced by hype. It draws its drama from context. Its long season tells the tale. If the World Series participants are not legitimate products of that long season's test, but instead the result of gimmickry, then the Series feels diminished.

This is no knock on Jim Leyland and the Marlins. They won the games they had to win, vanquishing the Braves in the NLCS. But the question nagged: If the Braves had proved themselves better than the Marlins over 162 games (and not by a bit, but significantly—nine games—better), why did they have to prove it again? The first question to ask is not whether a team *can* beat another team in the playoffs, because more so than in other sports anything can happen in a series in baseball (where an upset is statistically more likely than in any other sport). The first question is whether a team has *earned the right* to face another team in the playoffs. Prior to 1994, not every pennant or division winner was a great team, but they were all legitimate champions of distinct leagues or divisions, which validated the regular season and their inclusion in the postseason. Baseball plays 162 games to separate the good from the great, the pretenders from the contenders. So why let the pretenders get another shot?

1996: The absolute nadir. Conclusive proof that even when the truth jumps up and bites it, baseball remains oblivious. The Padres and Dodgers are not only tied after 161 games, they are playing each other on the season's final day. For a century, this would have defined the essence of baseball drama. After a season of twists and turns, everything rides on a single game. But now, in baseball's brave new world, the game carries zero significance. It is treated by both teams like an exhibition. Regulars are rested. Staff aces are held back. Why?

Neither team cared much whether it won the division or instead took the wild card. It was much more important to arrange their pitching rotations for the playoffs.

It is important to emphasize that the Padres–Dodgers situation was not a fluke. It is a fundamental flaw in a system riddled with flaws and contradictions. When you pick up the paper on August 1 and see that two teams are separated by a game atop any of baseball's divisions, you are kidding yourself if you begin to anticipate a pennant race between those teams. Unless, of course, it appears that they are both so mediocre that whichever team wins the division is likely to have a record worse than the wild-card team. Then and only then can a division race have the slightest excitement attached to it. Not only were the Dodgers and Padres playing for nothing in the last game of the season, but if you truly understood the system, you were deprived of even the anticipation of a great finish. You knew that no matter how close the standings may have appeared, the system precluded any high-end drama.

In any sport, the anticipation of what might happen is almost as important as what actually happens. For example, we know for a fact that only a tiny fraction of games are no-hitters, or are decided in the bottom of the ninth on a home run. Still the possibilities are tantalizing. But suppose you knew as a game unfolded that these outcomes were now impossible. That wouldn't just change how you felt in the ninth inning; it would change how you felt in the fourth and the fifth as well. You would be denied the anticipation of something memorable. That's what baseball has done to its pennant races. It has denied to all but the completely confused the true anticipation that a genuine pennant race might reach a stirring conclusion.

So the point here goes beyond saying that the wild card should be abolished just to preserve a few classic pennant-race finishes. Between 1969 and 1993 (discounting 1981's split season), there were 24 baseball seasons under the four-division system. That's nearly 100 divisional races, and in more than 60 percent of those races, the second-place team was within three games of the eventual champion sometime during September, keeping alive the possibility of a gripping conclusion.

1995: Entering the final day of the regular season, the Dodgers lead the Colorado Rockies by one game in the National League West, and yet the "race" is already over. The Dodgers have clinched the division and the Rockies, though in a position to tie them in the standings, have been declared the wild card. How? On the basis of a tiebreaker. The difference between winning the division and qualifying as the wild card is deemed so inconsequential that a playoff between the two would not take place in the event of a tie. Hence neither team cares about the final day's result.

Meanwhile, in the American League West, Seattle and California *do* tie for the division title. They do play a one-game playoff at the Kingdome, but only because both teams have a worse record than the wild-card qualifier, the New York Yankees. Therefore, the loser of the division race would be eliminated from the playoffs. The outcome matters only because it involves the fourth- and fifth-best teams in the league. Had they been any better than that, their "race" would have meant nothing.

The Angels, as you may recall, coughed up a big lead that year. But it did not have the feel of the epic pennant collapses of the past, because the wild card was there as a cushion. Only when the Yankees surged forward in the last weeks did the Angels–Mariners "race" take on any real significance.

1994: At the time of the strike in the beginning of August, the Texas Rangers lead the four-team American League West with a record ten games under .500, a mark that would have put them in last place in both of the American League's other two divisions. Yet they are playoff-bound. The single upside to the strike is that it probably saved baseball the embarrassment of a sub-.500 team in the playoffs. Admittedly, the wild card isn't to blame for this as much as the arbitrariness of a league with divisional splits in which everyone still plays an identical schedule, rather than a schedule weighted toward divisional opponents.

In the National League, the big story of the year—Felipe Alou's masterful job with the cash-poor Montreal Expos, and the Expos' decisive lead in the East division over the prohibitive favorite Atlanta Braves—was itself obscured by the wild card. The Expos' accomplishment was lessened because it wasn't definitive. Montreal would still have needed to vanquish Atlanta in the play-offs. For Atlanta's part, the fact that a team with a fraction of its payroll had soundly outplayed it through nearly three-fourths of the season was rendered meaningless. Atlanta hadn't really lost anything, since it still stood to qualify for the wild card.

In all of these years, we've seen yet another problem with the wild-card system. In addition to devaluing excellence and elevating mediocrity, in addition to depriving fans of classic pennant races, the wild card lacks an essential component of any sports drama:

Clarity.

While its presence undermines the entire season, its benefit, such as it is, doesn't even kick in until the very end when we can get a focus on which teams are vying for the wild-card spot while having no practical shot at the division title. Part of what always made pennant races interesting was that while they obviously carried their greatest excitement at the end, it was possible to follow them for an entire season. The ebb and flow of a true race for the pennant or division title was one of the unique pleasures of baseball. That's out the window now. So the wild card is a double whammy: You know from the start that its presence precludes a pennant race, but even on its own terms, it offers you little or nothing until the season's last week or so.

A few years back, while dismissing objections to the wild card as "traditionalist bull," David Cone complained that the '93 Giants, who won 103 games and lost the NL West by a game to Atlanta, "deserved" a chance at the postseason. Cone is a likable and in many ways admirable guy. But he's wrong on this one. The Giants *had* a chance at the postseason. One hundred and sixty-two chances. It was known as a pennant race. Just as it was in 1964 when the Cardinals, Phillies, Reds, and Giants came to the final weekend still alive. Or in the Red Sox' Impossible Dream season of 1967, when Boston, Minnesota, Chicago, and Detroit all had a shot at it right to the end. I don't recall anyone saying then, "Gee, wouldn't this be better, more exciting, if two or three of them could make it?" I don't recall a single base-ball fan saying in 1978 that it would have been better if both the Yankees and Red Sox had made the postseason and had dispensed with their silly little divisional race and one-game playoff at Fenway Park since, after all, they were both good teams and each "deserved" to be in the playoffs.

By the reckoning of those who defend the wild card, you'd somehow have twice as much drama if twice as many teams qualified for the playoffs. Those who accept that line of reasoning could just as well think that *Casablanca* would have been a better movie if there had been two Ingrid Bergmans. That way, one of them could have gone with Paul Henreid and the other could have stayed with Humphrey Bogart, and everyone would have been happy. (After all, both men "deserved" to win her love, right?)

So here's Russ Hodges's call of Bobby Thomson's home run if it happened today: "The Giants win the pennant!! The Giants win the pennant!! The Dodgers get the wild card!! The Dodgers get the wild card!!"

Inspiring, isn't it?

But rather than focusing on what has been lost, say wild-card proponents, you must focus on what has been gained, on what exciting developments have come about because of the wild card.

And here, all eyes turn toward the Mariners–Yankees wild-card series of 1995. This, more than any single thing, has served to shore up the wild card's support and confuse people about the system's merits.

Let's grant the obvious: The Yankees–Mariners series
was memorable. Five wild, exciting games, all won by the
home team, the last on an extra-inning hit that produced
the tying and winning runs and turned the Kingdome
into a madhouse. In addition, it was the Yankees' first
playoff appearance in 14 years. It was Seattle's first playoff appearance ever, and thus Ken Griffey Jr.'s first time
on the October stage. It was Don Mattingly's first and, as
it turned out, last crack at postseason play. And it was a
real chance for fans and, not incidentally, writers—in this
case New York writers—to revel in baseball on the field
after two years of bitter and alienating news surrounding
the game. In the giddy aftermath of that series, the following refrain was often heard, from announcers and
writers alike: "You know, I was skeptical before—but after
this series, how can you oppose the wild card?"

Huh?

These were five great baseball games. But the quality
of these games was not a product of the wild-card system.
That was coincidental. Consider this: Through 1999,
there have been 10 divisional series involving wild-card
teams, and other than Mariners–Yankees, none of them
made the slightest impact on the national consciousness.
Most fans outside the cities involved can't even recall
who played in most of them, let alone revisit any of the
game-by-game particulars. Clearly, proof of whether an
approach is good or bad cannot logically be found in any
one series.

Suppose that for one year baseball experiments with selecting the wild-card team out of a hat. Lo and behold, they pick the Cubs. A revived Kerry Wood throws a perfect game in the opener. Sammy Sosa clouts three homers and poets weep over the beauty of October baseball at Wrigley Field. Does this justify the Cubs' inclusion? Or simply serve to obscure its folly?

But surely there must have been some other benefits: The added round made for good TV, right? Check the ratings of the first-round division playoff games and you will find that they have been dismal by network standards, even when they involve big-market teams. Meanwhile, although several factors have affected the recent ratings of the World Series and League Championship Series, a strong case can be made that the additional round of playoffs has hurt them. More isn't better in this case. Baseball's postseason is taking on the feeling of a protracted tournament in which the World Series is becoming nothing more than the baseball finals. The big network money is derived from high World Series ratings. The fewer postseason games there are, the more special and meaningful each of them feels. Time will tell, but it seems likely that baseball's open-admission playoff format has only diminished its showcase event.

But what about attendance? Surely the prospect of the wild-card has boosted turnout in a number of cities that otherwise would be out of the race. This is another assertion that withers under examination. First, as we've detailed, the wild card eliminates at least as many races as it produces, often canceling out the divisional races, which otherwise would be more compelling. Logically that should cost attendance. Second, if you check the numbers, many of the teams in the wild-card chase would be in the race for first most of the season without the wild card. Wouldn't that engage their fans just as much or more? In terms of attendance, the wild card is at best a trade-off, and at worst an excitement killer. Down the stretch in '99, AL wild-card candidates Toronto and Oakland saw no attendance spike at all, and the NL wild-card contenders were in their respective division races for virtually the whole season anyway.

Now, the most recent argument in favor of the wild card goes something like this: The wild card is the only chance that medium-market teams have to compete, and so it's necessary in today's environment.

Two problems with this argument:

1. If it's true, then why not fix the main problem, that being today's environment, and the revenue inequity that leaves medium-market teams unable to compete?

2. It's not true in the first place. History teaches the opposite. The wild card has mainly given big-market clubs an additional chance to join the playoffs. If it gives anything to smaller-market teams, it's the *illusion* of a chance, because instead of chasing the first-place big-market club in their own division, they can instead hope to catch the second-place big-market club in someone else's division. And none of them has done so yet.

Here's a list of wild-card teams over the years, including the two clubs that would have qualified for the wild card in 1994 if the season ended at the point the strike occurred:

	American League	*National League*
1994	Cleveland	Atlanta
1995	NY Yankees	Colorado
1996	Baltimore	Los Angeles
1997	NY Yankees	Florida
1998	Boston	Chicago Cubs
1999	Boston	NY Mets

Where, pray tell, are the small- and middle-market teams? Every team in there fits one or more of four big-market groupings. And most teams that qualified had multiple advantages from this list: (1) a club in a large market, (2) a team with a big cable contract, (3) a team with a new stadium, or (4) the Florida Marlins, a team owned by a billionaire who spent like a "have" until he decided to sell the team and made it a "have-not."

The evidence is clear: The wild card offers a helping hand for the haves, not the have-nots.

But even if there weren't so much additional evidence condemning the wild card, there would still be the plain fact that it hurts pennant races. One of baseball's enduring strengths is its demanding regular season. Over the course of 162 games, we get a strong sense of the comparative abilities of teams. Except for aberrant seasons like the '62 Mets or the '98 Yankees, the best team will lose about 60 and the worst team will win about 60. Therefore, you need a long season to establish what, in terms of proportion, is really a relatively small difference. In fact, the difference between a pennant winner and a team that stinks is almost exactly the difference of winning the odd game of a seven-game series for most pennant-winning years. A team that loses four out of seven will win about 69 games in a season and be an also-ran. A team that wins four out of seven games over the course of a season will win about 93 games and likely contend for a title. And that, of course, is the nature of baseball, a sport where the differences between teams are not necessarily evident in one or two games.

Which is why it's all the more important for the regular season to separate the contenders from the pretenders.

In truth, given the nature of baseball, it is a practical impossibility to handicap the postseason in a way that justifies the inclusion of wild-card teams. (And consider this absurdity: If you qualify for the wild card from the same division as the team with the league's best record, you get a break—you don't have to play the league's best team in the first round. This may be a logical rule if there's going to be a wild card, because a division champion shouldn't have to begin the playoffs by playing a division foe it just beat over the course of a 162-game schedule. But this lesser of two evils is typical of the competitive conundrums that the wild card brings.)

Baseball, which once had the highest regard for its regular season, now sneers at it. It has gotten to the point where football, which plays a tenth as many games as baseball, takes its regular season much more seriously than the erstwhile national pastime. In football, if you have the best record in your conference, you receive enormous playoff advantages—a first-round bye and home-field advantage in *every* game (a home-field advantage that is obviously much more significant than in baseball). If you are a football wild-card team, you're at the other end of the spectrum, with an additional game, the toughest possible draw throughout, and a long road to the Super Bowl.

Contrast this with baseball. Everyone knows that a weaker team prefers to play a stronger club in a best-of-five crapshoot, rather than the truer best-of-seven test. And yet the division series, the only round guaranteed to include the wild card, is best-of-five. A team 20 games better than the wild-card enjoys no tangible advantage unless and until they meet in the fifth and decisive game of a series. And even there, the home-field edge in baseball means less than in any of the other team sports. Thus, not only is the wild card in the playoffs where it doesn't belong in the first place, it enters at no substantial disadvantage.

Wild-card proponents, as a last gasp, contend that the latest increase in the number of playoff teams is no different from the move to a divisional format in 1969, in which the number of playoff teams went from two to four. But the comparison is invalid. The divisional format may have taken some getting used to, but it preserved the essential elements of a pennant race. You had to finish first. And before the advent of the balanced schedule, the divisional races had complete integrity. All in all, the move made perfect sense: In the preceding decade, baseball had expanded from 16 teams to 24; practicality made four six-team divisions preferable to two 12-team divisions. And it passed the most important test of all: The Yankees versus the Orioles or Red Sox in the '70s, the Orioles–Brewers, Dodgers–Astros, Cardinals–Mets in the '80s, or the Braves–Giants in the '90s all felt like real pennant races.

It also had historical coherence. Bobby Thomson hit his 1951 home run in a straight pennant race. Bucky

Dent's dramatic 1978 homer at Fenway Park won a divisional race. They're both part of baseball's enduring legend. Because in both, as in all great pennant or divisional races, something big was at stake, something that could be won or lost forever by the narrowest of margins. That's what gave these moments their dramatic power. And it isn't just the winners who remain in your memory. Part of the beauty of the great pennant races was that the near misses were often as heartbreaking as the victories were exhilarating. In Philadelphia, the '64 Phillies, who let it all slip away, are as much a part of the city's history and collective psyche as the '80 Phils, who won it all.

Unforgettable moments like these, and countless pennant race moments that lead up to them, can never happen with the wild card. First of all, there are simply too many playoff spots to make winning any one of them nearly as important or prestigious as it once was. And the wild card provides a safety net that takes a huge element of drama away from regular-season play.

So in 1969, baseball went from two pennant races to four. In 1994, baseball went from four pennant races to none.

Baseball has feebly argued that it has fewer playoff teams than other sports, so what's the big deal about adding another tier, with four more teams? Here's the big deal: In basketball and hockey, where the regular season has never meant as much anyway, adding or reducing the number of playoff teams is only a matter of degree. Not so in baseball. The wild card changes the very nature of the thing. It's like arguing that you can somehow be just a little bit pregnant. Either you have a pennant race or you don't. And as long as you have even one wild card, you don't.

11

THE 3-AND-0 COUNT

So what do we do with the wild card? The assumption has been, since the very beginning, that with three divisions, you *must* have a wild card so that you'd have an even number of teams in the playoffs.

But free your mind for a moment and imagine the following: What if we just threw the wild card out?

You would still have three division races in each

league, and three division champions advancing to the playoffs. And then, come the playoffs, you'd deal with an odd number of playoff teams in each league by simply and appropriately giving the team with the best record in each league a bye into the League Championship Series.

While the other two division champions battle in a tense, best-of-five series to advance to the LCS, the team that posted the league's best mark would receive a just reward, getting a week to heal old wounds, put its pitching staff in order, and prepare for the best-of-seven match that will decide who advances to the World Series.

Now, as I've said before, I'm temperamentally more suited to the old alignment with two divisions in each league. But I'm also enough of a realist to know that baseball wants another tier of playoffs, and that if it were conducted right, TV might want this as well. With the three division champions, no wild card, and a bye, you don't lose that extra round of playoffs. And you gain the appeal of the first-round bye, a fruit of victory for the team that has performed the best in the long run of the regular season.

The great thing about the "3-and-0" solution is that it achieves, with a single stroke, multiple improvements in the competitive structure of the game. Just by eliminating the wild card and going with the bye, you are able to:

• Increase the value of the regular season by regaining the integrity of regular-season divisional races. Have

I harped on this point enough? Eliminating the wild card restores the value of the act of *qualifying* for the playoffs. No longer is there a sliding scale of excellence that allows merely good teams to advance and reduces the importance of winning any division.

• Increase the value of the regular season by increasing the number of teams eliminated in regular-season play. Just as the NFL (which eliminates 19 of 31 teams, or 61 percent of the competitors) has a more meaningful regular season than the NBA (which eliminates only 14 of 30 teams, or 46 percent), so it would be with baseball. A regular season that eliminates 24 of 30 teams simply accomplishes more—and thus means more—than a regular season that sees two fewer teams eliminated and two nonchampions advance.

• Increase the value of the postseason through the obvious corollary to the above rule. Since only six teams advance to the playoffs, the general quality of those teams is improved from the level of play when eight teams qualify. While there will still be some occasional pedestrian division champions advancing, there will be fewer clearly mediocre teams, like the '98 Cubs and Red Sox, or the '95 Rockies.

• Increase the value and drama of the regular season by increasing the number of clear-cut races in each league from zero to three—or, in actuality, four. You now not only have the three division races, untarnished and undiluted by the prospect of the wild card, but you also get the race for the overall best record and the all-important bye. Even in seasons in which one or two teams might be running away with their divisions, there's still a competition—for the bye. And unlike the side race surrounding the wild card, the competition for the bye would be among the two or three best teams in the league, not the fourth, fifth, and sixth.

• Increase the value of the regular season and the playoffs by more clearly increasing the graduated post-season rewards that accrue to the best teams over the course of the regular season. Rather than the best record in the league getting you merely an extra home game the first two rounds, it now gives you a free pass to the LCS *and* home-field advantage. And, of course, the bye has an added value in baseball. In addition to being able to nurse injuries, which might be true in any sport, in baseball you can get your pitching rotation in order.

Having the second-best record among division winners would still carry an advantage, since it would provide home-field edge for that first-round series. Winners advance to the LCS, losers walk. That's the case now, of course, but the series has less definition, since the second-seeded team isn't always playing the third-seeded team (they play the fourth seed when the wild card is in the same division as the division champion with the best overall record). Also, a single first-round series in each league would *feel* different, partially because it would get more attention and also because the next round's opponent would already be known. The objective is clearer, and the outcome is guaranteed to have credibility. Either the team with the best record and the bye wins the LCS, authenticating its standing and place in the World Series, or it loses to a team that has defeated that league's other two division champions to get to the Series. There is no easy or lucky way around it. No chance that the World Series will feel, as it did in 1997, like the finals of a bloated and convoluted tournament.

• Increase the value of the playoffs for both fans and TV networks. There would be fewer total playoff games, but the games that are played would be more important, and there would be greater focus on those contests. Rather than the diffuse, underwhelming system of four different series going on in a single week, there would never be more than two series being played at any one time.

Baseball could return to its old schedule of starting the first-round series a day apart, then switching off between prime-time and day games. Each series would hold the attention of fans, because you'd have a chance, as in the pre-'94 era, to follow all the postseason games played.

• Finally, what the 3-and-0 solution really gets you, in spades, is clarity. Let's go back to 1999, when the

Cincinnati Reds chased the Houston Astros, and the New York Mets chased the Atlanta Braves for much of the summer. Because of the wild card, these two division races involving those four teams was really a single clumped-together race in which three teams would advance and only one would be eliminated.

On the morning of September 20, with two weeks to go in the season, the standings looked like this:

NL Central	W	L	GB	NL East	W	L	GB
Houston	92	59	—	Atlanta	93	57	—
Cincinnati	88	62	3½	New York	92	58	1

With no wild card, you'd not only have two great clear-cut division races, but you'd also have an equally clear side race, among the division leaders (last year also involving Arizona, which was just a game off Atlanta's pace), for the crucial one-week bye. And it stands to reason that the tighter and more demanding the pennant race, the more important it would be to win the bye along with the division.

What do you lose in all this? You'd lose the welfare-state illusion that allows teams playing around .500 at the All-Star break the shameless luxury of teasing themselves and their fans with talk of getting back into the wild-card picture.

You would lose the bogus argument that being in a wild-card race somehow brings out more fans. (Oakland, having its best season in years in 1999, was drawing 18,000 per game, though it was in the wild-card picture most of the way.)

What else? Inevitably, some would complain about the bye, arguing that the best team would face the prospect of being rusty come the League Championship Series. But this is a false issue. In a knockout tournament, in which each round includes the risk of elimination, any rational manager or player would prefer to take the free pass and risk possible "rustiness" rather than risk elimination, injury, or a scrambled pitching rotation in the pursuit of the next round.

And you wouldn't have to be rusty. Open your home stadium during the week of the first-round playoffs, and play some intrasquad games, or games against your own minor leaguers. Play them under true game conditions, with major league umpires and all the rest. Charge a buck or two, and give all ticket proceeds to a local youth group or athletic organization. Rally the fans, and give everyone a chance to bask in the glory of regular-season triumph before getting down to the serious business of the LCS.

Ultimately, what you'd have by eliminating the wild card and adding the bye is an ultramodern three-division setup that still had the contours of the old pennant races. Six legitimate division champions, plus more side races for byes and home-field advantages. Then a brutal knock-out series in each league, among division champions, each trying to advance to the LCS. Interest, tension, and pressure building up to the World Series and a sense, come the Fall Classic, that the participants are more than arbitrary survivors—they are, in fact, true champions. As they should be.

It would be modern and yet timeless. Innovative yet classic. Baseball's past and baseball's future.

12

LOOSE ENDS

We've come this far. So let's finish the work.

Now we're ready to argue about the designated hitter and a few other items. The DH question has received disproportionate attention in baseball's debates over the past decade. Not that this isn't a legitimate question, but it's a bit like the critic who reviewed Nero's fiddling while

Rome burnt to the ground—an interesting case, but rather beside the point.

Once you get the economics sorted out, and return meaningful pennant races to the regular season, you then can take up the narrower but still important issues.

THE DH

Proponents of the designated hitter rule can say what they want. But they can't contest this fact: The best games of the '99 postseason, between the Mets and Braves, were infinitely more interesting because the NL doesn't use the DH. The moves and countermoves that Bobby Cox and Bobby Valentine made in those games were predicated on the judicious use of pitchers and their accompanying spot in the order. If those games are played under AL rules, there are a dozen fewer lineup changes, a much less intriguing battle of wits, and, in the end, significantly less drama. This doesn't mean a genius is needed to execute a double switch, only that the strategy brought into the game by making the pitcher hit adds a texture and complexity worth preserving.

But that's not the only, and perhaps not even the best, reason to jettison the DH. Quite simply, the designated hitter rule provides a solution for a problem that no longer exists. Though I was never a fan of the DH, I understood that—unlike the wild card—there were reasonable arguments for it. I felt the weight of evidence still worked against it, but I was never outraged by it. It has provided a way for stars like Al Kaline, Paul Molitor, and Darryl Strawberry to extend their careers, and that has undeniable appeal.

But apart from this, every argument that's ever been made for the existence of the DH not only doesn't compel any longer, it's been turned on its head. The AL is not chasing the NL for fans' interest the way it was in the late '60s and early '70s, when the Yankee dynasty lay in ruins and the National League was brimming with stars, many of them black and Hispanic players that AL clubs had been generally slow to sign.

And in terms of offense, which was to be resuscitated by the DH, we can safely say that the patient is ready to breathe without life support. In the early '70s, baseball was still recovering from an offensive famine. A batting title was won at .301 in 1968. An entire league batted .239 in the '72 season. Home-run titles could be won with figures in the low 30s. In 1968, 21 percent of all games were shutouts. Now, a generation later, batters are stronger, ballparks and strike zones are smaller, pitching is stretched thinner. So offense is way up—actually reaching the point of distortion in the AL, to say nothing of Colorado.

Oddly, it is around the issue of the DH where baseball has shown commendable foresight and resource-fulness. In '97, the owners proposed to the Players Association that the DH be phased out over time, with a permanent extra roster spot added in return. This offer is so fair and reasonable, the Players Association ought to be embarrassed to have rejected it. It's further proof (as if any were needed) that the Players Association, which once fought for fair and honorable goals, is now often committed to little more than the narrowest self-interest. Most DHs make high salaries, and that apparently trumps all other considerations, including the quality of the game and 30 extra jobs for the union.

THE ALL-STAR GAME

Even with interleague play and constant player movement diminishing its appeal, baseball's summer event is still sport's best all-star spectacle, and nothing else is even close. Two things that would further improve it:

Expand the rosters to 32, and eliminate the rule that says each team must be represented. It makes sense for each *host* team to have a representative, but in a world of 30 major league teams, the each-team-represented rule wreaks too much havoc with rosters, forcing managers to eliminate a better player, or take a bad team's second- or even third-best player because he fits a position.

INTERNATIONAL DRAFT

The time has come. It's pointless to continue letting a few teams like the Yankees and Dodgers bid on the likes of every Orlando Hernandez and Hideki Irabu who comes down the pike. Standardize the system, and encourage teams to start scouting worldwide. Then incorporate the international draft into the amateur draft, but make it a worldwide draft.

This will accomplish a couple of things: First, it will level the playing field in terms of player acquisition, meaning that the teams that do the best scouting will again be best rewarded. Second, it will force every franchise to be aggressive in finding new markets for talent. At a time when baseball's outreach program is trying to tap into Latin America and Asia, this makes a lot of sense. More important than a couple of regular-season games in Japan are scouts working around the world to bring the best players to this country—just as international hockey scouting has done in the NHL.

UMPIRES

History will show that reform-minded Sandy Alderson has the right idea, just as it's already shown that deposed umpires union chief Richie Phillips had the wrong one. Alderson, MLB's executive vice president, moved last year to centralize the umpiring system under the umbrella of the commissioner's office. Though the umps rebelled, they were blind on this one. Officiating will never be perfect, but leagues like the NFL and NBA work hard to make sure the crews they put out on the field or court are accountable and held to the highest possible standards. There's a constant review process, and the weakest are weeded out. Baseball's ancient system has encouraged a vocal minority of umps to believe they're bigger than the game. What rational person opposes the idea that umpires be required to be in good physical shape? Who thinks it's a good idea for some umpires to be so belligerent that they not only prolong but in some cases instigate disputes?

And why don't umps seek help on anything more important than a checked swing? In other sports, officials are encouraged to confer if necessary. In baseball, where there is a strange code of self-reliance, this is virtually never done.

Finally, umpires have brainwashed too many people into thinking it's somehow okay to call a ridiculously wide or ridiculously low strike zone, "just as long as it's consistent." What umpires should strive for is to consistently be right. When a team's pitching strategy changes depending on which man in blue is calling balls and strikes, the umpires need to be reined in. You never hear Al Michaels say "the officials are calling a wide sideline tonight." You don't hear Marv Albert say, "It's a short three-pointer today." So why should baseball stand for this nonsense, just because it has in the past?

Enforcing the rule-book strike zone would have important additional effects. First, it would allow pitchers a better chance to get ahead in the count, quickening the pace of games. Baseball's once-leisurely pace was an asset. Its now-often-lethargic pace is a problem. Additionally, it would slow the alarming increase in scoring.

All these common-sense corrections should and likely will take place under Alderson's leadership.

INSTANT REPLAY

It makes sense to use technology, when appropriate, to get an important call right. But the only time it should be used in baseball is in the postseason. Baseball's regular-season games are televised with wide variations of camera coverage and production expertise—and in many cases are covered by crews with obvious ties to a particular team. So uniformity and evenhandedness cannot be achieved during the regular season. Plus, over 162 games, things have a way of evening out.

Not so come October, where every play is magnified, and every game is staffed by network crews with so many cameras, they can devote one just to shooting Leo Mazzone.

The approach here should be simple. Instant replay should be used solely at the discretion of the umpiring crew, or a supervisor assigned to the game. It should be used to overrule a call only in cases where there is conclusive visual evidence that a mistake was made. Obviously, it shouldn't be used on balls and strikes. Used sensibly, this would provide a way to correct the outrageously bad calls, like the phantom double play that killed the Red Sox in Game 1 of the ALCS in '99, or the blown call at first base that hurt the Cardinals in Game 6 of the 1985 World Series.

MINORITIES AND BASEBALL

Every sport has an old boys network, and in baseball, most of the old boys are white. The irony is that baseball's racial makeup on the field is so pluralistic.

Commissioner Bud Selig is right to require teams to at least honestly consider minorities when they have field manager or front-office positions open. But that prescriptive alone isn't likely to open any closed minds or doors. What's also needed is the same sort of oversight and commitment at the minor league level, both for uniformed and front-office personnel. Even more than in the past, this will be the major league's feeder system, for two reasons: (1) Most modern players make so much money, they're less likely to want to spend three years in Huntsville grooming for a big-league bench job; and (2) the job description for general managers has changed to include qualifications beyond baseball background and talent evaluation.

Looking farther into the future, what the sport also needs to do is put even more money into the inner cities and make baseball a hot urban sport again. There's a smaller percentage of African-Americans playing in major league baseball than in either the NBA or the NFL. And this has everything to do with the pool of players coming from high school and colleges: A study by the *Austin American-Statesman* in the mid-'90s showed that only 3% of college baseball players were African-American. More high schools need varsity baseball programs, and more youth centers need the equipment and space to play baseball.

The owners and players have shown positive signs of coming together on this one, with far-sighted programs that encourage participation and interest in baseball among youth in general and inner-city kids in particular. There's still more to be done: For less than the annual cost of a utility infielder, each major league club could significantly bolster youth baseball programs in its area. It's the future of the game.

PETE ROSE

I know, I know. Fans are forever calling talk shows to make the point that drug users, wife-beaters, and miscreants of every sort are given second, third, and seventh chances by baseball, while poor Pete Rose sits on the outside looking in, a victim of baseball's zero-tolerance policy on gambling. I understand the sentiment, but not the logic. All sports (and especially baseball, since the 1919 Black Sox scandal) make a valid distinction between gambling and other misdeeds that may in fact be as bad or worse elsewhere in society, but don't in the mere act of commission bring into question the integrity of the sport itself. No one believes any longer that sports and all of its participants are pure. However, we are still able to believe in the basic honesty of the contests themselves. When that is called into question, there is no product to sell. Baseball has made that clear for generations. Everybody in the game knows it. Pete Rose knew it.

Still, even if you believe every line of John Dowd's report on Rose's wrongdoings, and convincing stuff it is, there isn't a whiff of speculation that he ever committed the cardinal sin in sports of betting against his own team. Betting on *any* baseball game should carry a significant penalty. Betting on a game in which you're involved, even if you're betting on your own team, should carry a stiffer penalty still. It's a very serious offense. But so is armed robbery, and yet we make a distinction between that and murder. So should a distinction be made between betting on your team and betting against it. One is surely a felony, but the other is a capital offense. And yet baseball's written rules make no distinction between betting on your own team in April, and throwing the seventh game of the World Series.

Rose deserved a lengthy suspension. You can make a case that he still deserves to be banned from the game 10 years later, especially in the absence of any real contrition. But one that seems harder to argue is that Rose should still be banned from eligibility for the Hall of Fame. The after-the-fact 1991 ruling that barred players on baseball's ineligible list from the Hall was clearly passed to prevent Rose from getting his due. The result is that the issue is now needlessly complicated by the coupling of Rose's ban from baseball with his ineligibility for the Hall. The two need to be considered separately. If they are, virtually all the controversy surrounding this issue disappears. If Pete gets into the Hall but remains banned from baseball, justice will have been tempered by both common sense and mercy, with no possible inference that baseball had suddenly gone soft on gambling. Ten years and counting? That's not a deterrent?

So by now, he should be back on the ballot. His transgressions might prevent him from being elected to the Hall on the first ballot, but he would make it eventually. And he deserves to be there, with his baseball achievements immortalized on a plaque that also makes note of his banishment from the game for gambling.

COMMERCIALISM

There are a couple of things that ought to remain sacred in baseball. One is the uniform. It's one thing for an athletic manufacturer's logo to appear at the bottom of the sleeve. But this talk of selling space for corporate advertising is unseemly and crass, unless your idea of a great sports event is the Goody's Headache Powder 500.

The best-run leagues understand that what they should be marketing primarily is the game itself. It's fine to pitch whatever you want between innings, but if you're a baseball man, the only thing you want fans thinking about when Randy Johnson faces Chipper Jones is Randy Johnson facing Chipper Jones, not the behind-the-plate advertising rotating from batteries to beer.

During the game is not the time to sell anything but baseball. And if baseball keeps to this, it will remain compelling enough that there will be plenty of opportunity to sell those other things, and plenty of customers to sell them to.

Television and radio can do their part by resisting the urge to freight every piece of information it gives fans, from starting lineups to statistical roundups to scouting reports, with corporate advertising. When I see that ESPN Sunday Night Baseball is "presented by Gumout," all I can think is, "Isn't it being presented by ESPN?" And if, in fact, that's the Budweiser Starting Lineup I'm reading on NBC, did August Busch III fill it out, or was that still left up to Joe Torre?

Moreover, the implicit assumption of selling commercial space on jerseys and the like—that all-consuming need for more revenue from every possible source—has been revealed for what it is earlier in this book. Fans are right to sneer at it. Players, who ought to be sensitive to the way they're perceived, shouldn't stand for it. And owners shouldn't ask for it.

People say, "Yeah, but where do you draw the line on advertising?" Let's draw it right here: No advertising on uniforms, no advertising on foul poles, and—please—no more advertising behind home plate.

THE FALL CLASSIC

Everything I've argued in this book up to this point is, I believe, rooted in logic. The plans for the game's future are made in a real-world context, and can be defended on rational grounds rather than just idealistic ones.

So let me make just one case for aesthetics.

The World Series always follows a Saturday-Sunday/Tuesday-Wednesday-Thursday/Saturday-Sunday format, and for more than a decade, all of these games have been night games, because television wants it to justify the high rights fees that baseball wants. (And, for the most part, that's fine, although I won't defend starting East Coast games as late as 8:20 P.M.)

Playing most World Series games at night makes perfect sense, because it gives more people a chance to see the games. But there's an indefinable something about having one or two of these games played during the day. There are few settings in sports more appealing than a ballpark on a sunny October afternoon, with bunting along the railings and Series combatants on the field. It's attractive in and of itself, but it also connects the modern game to eras past, which is not just the concern of the nostalgic but an important part of the game's ongoing identity.

So what if you did this: Play one day game in each team's park. Make them Game 1 and Game 4, and start them at 3 P.M. eastern. So you begin the World Series in a classic atmosphere on Saturday afternoon, setting a certain tone while sacrificing Saturday's prime time, where viewership levels are generally the lowest of the week. You move back to prime time for Game 2 on Sunday night, when viewership is high.

Now on to the next city for the middle games of the Series. With Games 3 and 4 played Tuesday night and Wednesday afternoon, think of the subtle ways that might add to the strategic considerations of player use for each manager. Better still, think of people heading home from work, picking up the game on the radio, and arriving at home in time to see the last couple of innings on TV. Think of the way some kids (not all, as before, but still a large proportion) would be buzzing in school on that Wednesday afternoon, trying to sneak a peek at the game, or hurrying home after the end of classes. Thirty years ago, they'd bring transistors into the classrom. In this day and age, maybe they'd sneak into their computer lab and log on to ESPN.com to follow the GameCast, or something like that. But you get the idea.

We go back to prime time for Games 5, 6, and 7, where audience levels naturally grow as the Series builds toward its conclusion.

Moving these two games to the late afternoon would

cost the sport something in rights fees (since it would cost the networks something in advertising revenues). But it would add texture to the Series, since these games would look and feel different, and be recalled with a different visual shorthand. And it would generate, among the community of baseball fans, the goodwill that comes with something that feels right for all the right reasons.

Now let me snap out of this little reverie and acknowledge that the idea of two Series day games almost certainly will not fly. With no more than four games guaranteed, we'd be asking baseball and its network partners to pull as much as half of any given Series out of prime time. But let's look at this like a negotiation. You ask for more than you're likely to get, and hope to come out ahead of where you started. While Saturday *and* Wednesday day games may be a reach, playing the Saturday opener in sunshine makes perfect sense.

And even with this single nod to aesthetics, the point would have been made, on baseball's very center stage, that the sport exists for reasons beyond the maximizing of profits for owners and players—that it is more than just entertainment, and more than merely a business.

And for those who might have grown cynical or indifferent about the game, if they were to reconsider and look at it again on one October afternoon, they'd realize something: that it is still baseball, a game that has evolved and modernized over the past few decades, but still essentially the same game we fell in love with as kids. A game that can still serve as a common ground across generations.

And a game that, revived and rededicated, can prosper for generations to come.

CONCLUSION

Where do we go from here?

Following the 2001 season, the owners and the players will have to hammer out a new contract.Can you imagine anything more excruciating than having to sit through the same tired posing and machinations that we've seen and heard so often in the past? While push is likely to come to shove between the 2001 and 2002 seasons, it is imperative that the owners come together well before that, spelling out their plan so that all parties may consider and debate it before the 11th hour.

Commissioner Bud Selig, given broad new powers early in 2000, must use these powers not merely to identify but to forge an unshakable consensus among the owners that significant revenue-sharing is essential. More piecemeal "solutions" like the luxury tax hammered out in 1995 would be disastrous. The revenue-sharing plan they arrive at must be not only far-reaching, but also tied to larger principles that will hold even as the dollar figures change in the years ahead.

No one should underestimate the practical difficulties involved, given baseball's historically acrimonious factions, not just between owners and players but among the owners themselves. And realistically, much of what has been proposed here would need to be phased in over a period of years.

But if hardball must be played, then play it. If it means that the Kansas Citys and Pittsburghs of the world tell the New Yorks that when they go on the road to the small-market stadiums, they won't be allowed to plug in their TV equipment, then so be it. If it means telling them that they can show up in spring training by themselves, because the vast majority of teams won't be there, that's fine, too. This is the time and place for them to draw the line.

By the same token, the rank and file of the Players Association needs to realize that the sacred cow of unlimited wages now only serves to slow overall salary growth and destabilize the entire game. They must stop viewing all suggestions that a dysfunctional system needs reform as an assault on their most basic rights. And they've got to come together and recognize that only through payroll ceilings *and floors* will the general well-being of most players be served. Can a union really pass on substantial overall salary gains just so the top five percent of players can continue testing the boundaries of market sanity? Now's the time for them to take the high road, and contribute constructive thoughts toward a plan that makes sense for a majority of players *and* stabilizes the economics of the game.

Do I think these things will happen? Maybe not, given the history of bumbling and duplicity on one side and intransigence on the other. But this much is undeniable: We have arrived at a time when a majority of owners and a majority of players have something in common: a strong incentive to correct the overall system, before it prices even more teams out of contention and, in the process, consigns even more players to the netherworld of those teams' rosters. Or, worse still, forces some teams out of business entirely, taking those big-league jobs with them.

So here's hoping that common sense will prevail. In the past two years, we've seen the NBA come to its senses and realize—even though the league was ostensibly healthy—where things were headed. The owners decided to slam on the brakes before driving off the cliff. They shut their game down, not in the purposeless way in which baseball burned its World Series of 1994, but with a clear, tough vision of what the sport should be as well as what it would become if they did not act decisively. Throughout much of the '98–'99 NBA lockout, the following was heard from all sectors of the media and fans: *Didn't they learn anything from baseball?*

But as I said at the time, those observers had the question exactly backward. The question should have been and now is, *What has baseball learned from basketball?* Are the vast majority of clubs who cannot continue under this system willing to be tough enough and far-sighted enough to do what is necessary to set it straight?

I hope so. They need to be willing to shut the game down again, if necessary, until the big-market high-rollers among the owners and the idealogues among the players see that there simply will not be any baseball played until a workable economic system is in place. When the NBA showed the brains and resolve to go that route, some pundits claimed that the basketball players—whose union was neither as strong nor as capably directed as the baseball players'—had merely capitulated. And yet the salaries of average players went up almost immediately, as did the pay of journeyman benchwarmers. The sole "negative" consequence to the players is that Stephon Marbury and Keith Van Horn must scrape by on about $10 million per year instead of $15 million.

The fact is that if the owners play their hand right, the biggest difference between the basketball situation and what should happen in baseball is simply how long it will likely take before the players see that the owners have their act together and mean business.

It will be a long, hard road. But it has to be taken. The responsibility for change ultimately falls on the owners. They are the caretakers of the game. They are the ones who must take the lead in reshaping it. And they are the ones who will be blamed if the next work stoppage doesn't bring about meaningful and lasting changes.

And what about the fans? They need to do what the owners and players have so often been incapable of doing: See the big picture, knowing that if this plays out as it might, sacrificing some or even all of the 2002 season will be well worth it if baseball finally establishes some equilibrium.

We can at least hope that, in this age of instant gratification, baseball will awaken to the idea that some things that may cost a bit of revenue in the short term are actually an investment in the game's popularity and prosperity in the long-term. Players and owners alike need to be less willing to sacrifice the game's essence on the altar of commercialism.

If they come to this realization, they will have our gratitude, our respect, and our continued support. And I promise you that all those involved will be richer in the long run.

SOME PARTING THOUGHTS

The 2000 baseball season ended as the one before it had—with the jubilant New York Yankees celebrating in their clubhouse, George Steinbrenner commending Joe Torre on the fine job he did in handling the pressures of repeating, and the talk of dynasty in the air. Come the off-season, the Yankees reloaded again, snatching Mike Mussina, the top pitcher on the free-agent market.

One can respect and admire the Yankees' resiliency, professionalism, and effective use of their overwhelming resources and still not lose sight of the bigger picture, as some apparently have. In the aftermath of the team's fourth title in five years, one postgame commentator actually said that the latest run by the Bronx Bombers is all the more amazing because dynasties are harder to achieve in the free-agency era. This statement was true in the free-agency years *prior* to the 1994–95 strike (when only one team repeated over a 15-year stretch and multiple teams from every market and revenue level were represented among the winners and contenders). But it has been patently un-true *since* the strike, when all six titles have been won by teams with payrolls among the top five in baseball, and 10 of the 12 World Series participants have been among the top five (even the other two were seventh and tenth).

There's something worth clarifying here: While the Yankees' recent World Series wins and ever-increasing revenue and payroll advantages have served to crystallize baseball's competitive imbalance crisis, the real problem is not that the Yankees have won so often, but that so many other teams have no reasonable chance to win at all. So even if the Yankees had been tripped up in a play-off or World Series now and then, you'd have a different world champion but not a different essential conclusion.

A word for those who continue to insist that it has "always" been like this: It hasn't. The Yankees dynasty of past decades was a product of much different circumstances and, in any case, had ground to a halt more than a decade before the advent of free agency. In the NL, the stretch of Cardinal and Dodger success in the '40s and '50s was a product of Branch Rickey's visionary development of the farm system and, in the case of the Dodgers, his even greater vision concerning integration. When those justly gained runs of excellence subsided in the mid-'50s, check the National League winners and contenders thereafter. It's a varied list.

Still, excellence or even dominance is not inherently troubling. Under the right conditions, fans welcome it and celebrate it. The key question is how it's attained. When Michael Jordan's Bulls won six out of eight NBA titles (and six of six when he played the full season), there was none of the sense of predestined resignation that has greeted the latest Yankees dynasty. There were no calls to change the structure of the NBA. The Bulls earned their dynasty the old-fashioned way, through savvy, patience, and a little good luck. They got Jordan in the draft, after Portland had passed him over; down the road, they made a draft-day trade to get Scottie Pippen. They added key role players based on basketball judgment. These were moves made in the normal process of personnel acquisition, not a case of a team buying a competitive advantage that the vast majority of other clubs could never afford.

Meanwhile, in baseball: Alex Rodriguez signs a free-agent contract valued at $252 million, nearly twice the estimated value of the *entire Oakland Athletics franchise,* and greater than the estimated value of 18 of the 30 major league clubs. In the midst of all the gnashing of teeth and rending of garments over the sheer enormity of the numbers, there is an essential point that some continue to miss. We still hear the old line that "as long as owners are willing and able to spend this kind of money, there must not be any real problem. We'll know they can't afford it when they stop paying it." That line of thinking is perfectly valid as long as a substantial majority of the owners are able to spend that kind of money. But we are now in an environment in which only a *handful* of owners can make this type of player investment. And the impact of all this on the game itself is too powerful to ignore.

Not only are the A-Rods and Mike Hamptons out of

reach for a majority of teams, but what those players are paid dictates the market for roughly comparable players elsewhere, regardless of market size or revenue potential. Good luck to the A's trying to keep Jason Giambi. Royals fans already know they can't expect a contender; now they know they shouldn't get too attached to Johnny Damon either. Of course, when players such as these move on, their agents invariably intone, "My guy would have loved to stay. It wasn't about the money. He just wants to be with a contender." Yes, we know.

For true competition to exist, you must have some reasonable equality of opportunity. Not equality of results; not every team hovering around .500 or 30 different World Series winners over the next 30 years. Just a reasonable opportunity to build *and maintain* a contending team with good management and a little luck. That opportunity exists in the other major team sports. While the Yankees were in the midst of their late-'90s run through Big Market Baseball, the San Antonio Spurs won an NBA title and the Green Bay Packers went to back-to-back Super Bowls. No one believes the team from tiny Green Bay is at a significant competitive disadvantage relative to the Giants or Jets, but everyone knows that just down the road, the Milwaukee Brewers—with or without a new stadium—might as well be on a different planet from the Yankees or Mets.

Now, those who took issue with *Fair Ball* argued that the developments of the 2000 season offered "proof" that the plans outlined in the book weren't needed. A question

I heard more than once: *Didn't the rise of the Chicago White Sox and Oakland Athletics prove that payroll disparity doesn't really matter all that much?*

In a word, no. It's nice to see the underdogs rise up, and the gritty performances of the Athletics and White Sox were heartening. But their success is largely an anomaly. The White Sox are a big-market team with a small-market payroll; they could well afford to increase it and soon will have to. In the case of the Athletics, there are two obvious reasons that their success doesn't change the thesis: 1) I've never said that, against all odds, a team couldn't catch lightning in a bottle in a single given year and use a nucleus of young, relatively affordable players to make a run at a title, especially in an era of multiple mini-divisions. What I did say, and will continue to say, is that no small-market team can hope to keep such a squad together or hope to consistently contend in the present environment. 2) It's amusing to see those who remain unwilling to come to terms with the present realities grasping at whatever straws they can (A's, White Sox) while ignoring the mountain of evidence that points in the opposite direction. The numbers tell the true story: Since the strike, teams in the top half of payrolls have won 186 playoff games; teams in the bottom half have won three games. Teams in the top half of payrolls won 24 postseason series. Teams in the bottom half won precisely zero. I'm no sabermetrician, but I think I've spotted a trend here.

So the essential state of baseball has remained unchanged—or if anything, grown worse—in the year since
Fair Ball was first published.

Now, more than ever, I find the points and arguments
made in *Fair Ball* echoed elsewhere. I'd been making some
of those points on the air for several years. But pulling them
all together in one place, between hard covers, seems to
have afforded them a different sort of consideration. Of
course I had hoped that would be the case, but I wondered
if a book essentially about policy could find an audience. As
it turned out, it did, and I think the reason is simple: The
issues that had concerned me for a long time have now
become so pressing that they resonate with the average fan.

And we are not alone. The book arrived in stores in late
April 2000, shortly after Major League Baseball floated a
preposterous trial balloon on realignment that would have
had four four-team divisions and no wild card in one league
and three divisions (two fives and a four) with the wild card
in the other league. But by the middle of the season, even
the Players Association and some national columnists were
pitching plans similar to the scenario outlined here, in
which the Astros would move to the AL West. Any support
for the cockamamie 16–14 scheme had faltered.

In July, the Commissioner's Blue Ribbon Panel on Baseball Economics (which included Yale president Richard C.
Levin, former Federal Reserve Board chairman Paul A.

Volcker, former Maine senator George Mitchell, and columnist George Will) released its findings, including the call for greater revenue sharing and a salary floor, with an estimate of a $40 million minimum team payroll.

Rather than the defined ceiling I proposed, the panel recommended a luxury tax of 50 percent on all payrolls that advanced beyond $84 million. I'm skeptical of the long-term success of such a plan, since it would allow the rich to continue spending vastly more money than other teams in the league. Still, when combined with more revenue sharing and a salary floor, it is infinitely better than the present system. And it would at least guarantee that a team that wanted to buy a World Series would have a more difficult time doing so.

I have other issues with the Blue Ribbon Panel's report. For example, I find it hard to believe its conclusion that only three teams made a profit in 1999. But in terms of the principles that should guide a league and the framework for change, we're on the same page.

And we've got company: More and more, from the sports pages to the op-ed pages, we see growing support for the idea that no public funds should be committed for new ballparks until baseball reforms its internal economics. *The New York Times* called for some form of revenue sharing and salary restraint on its editorial page last December, and Harvard law professor Paul C. Weiler's book *Leveling the Playing Field: How the Law Can Make Sports Better for Fans* floated similar recommendations.

Even Andrew Zimbalist, long a Players Association ally, has expressed the view that the arguments that applied prior to 1994 are no longer relevant and that a new model—one calling for concessions by both players and owners—is needed.

Just as telling are the perspectives of onetime Players Association activists who later became managers or front-office executives—Joe Torre, Don Baylor, Sal Bando, Ted Simmons, and others. They were there when the Players Association had its finest hours, fighting for real and enduring principles. They'd never want to turn back the clock. Still, they've seen the situation as it's evolved from both sides now and recognize that if you're going to have a *league* working anything like a *league* should, you've got to look forward and make some practical adjustments.

Believe me, I'm aware of all the arguments that once supported the players' position and refuted the owners'. For the most part, I agreed with those arguments. But the landscape has changed so dramatically that those points either no longer apply or carry less weight than they once did. Only the inattentive or the doctrinaire infer that I've taken the "owners' side." I'm on the side of what makes sense for the game.

Almost any person who's given the topic serious thought realizes the system needs an overhaul. This is now so obvious, the evidence for it so clear and overwhelming, that only those with a transparent vested interest in maintaining the dysfunctional status quo could possibly argue otherwise.

Which brings us to the leaders of the Players Association.

"Baseball's attendance and revenues are at an all-time high," said Marvin Miller. "The game has never been more prosperous. For George Will, George Mitchell, and Bob Costas to suggest that baseball has a competitive balance problem is absurd."

The truth is that the real absurdity in this case is the unbending stance of the Players Association and their willful blindness to the larger issues affecting the game. They have been arguing their rhetoric for so long (and so effectively) that they have either become oblivious to the massive changes in baseball's circumstances or decided it would be a tactical error to concede even an inch of the argument to management.

As this book plainly states, and as the Blue Ribbon Panel observed, baseball's *overall* revenues and attendance are larger than ever and still growing. And under the present system, this is part of the problem, not part of the solution. The problem, as everyone who isn't still fighting the battles of the '60s and '70s knows, is revenue distribution and competitive balance. Baseball's vast revenues give it the wherewithal to get well, if the owners and players want to make it happen.

While my sense is that for the most part the press is finally moving toward a more accurate take on all this, there are still times when the media contributes to misunderstanding. For example, this observation (or something close to it) has appeared in countless publications: "Don Fehr and the players have long scoffed at the owners' claims of poverty." While that is true, it's also misleading. Because any claims of owner "poverty" (or, more accurately, annual losses) is largely beside the point. Although it might reasonably be asked why anyone should begrudge owners substantial returns on substantial investments, the bottom line of even the least wealthy owner is not our concern here. What is our concern is that team's ability to compete on the field. We assume that, as we have seen, teams will adjust their operating expenses based on how much their owners wish to make or are willing to lose. In the end, as individuals, the owners will be just fine. But great wealth in absolute terms is not the same thing as great wealth in relative terms. And relative strength is what sports is all about.

Think of it this way: If you and I play a game of Monopoly, and you start out staked to a million dollars plus Boardwalk and Park Place, and I get a hundred grand and Baltic Avenue, and if at the end of the game, I have $200,000, I've clearly made a profit. In one sense I've clearly done well. But at no point did I have any real chance to *win the game*. And anyone watching the game would have known that from Go.

Even if all 30 teams were profitable, that still wouldn't get anywhere near the heart of the problem. Just because some clubs slash their payrolls and show a yearly profit, or others come out ahead on equity, doesn't mean baseball's problems are solved.

In fact, if we could toss aside the blinders imposed by decades of precedent and partisan posturing, we'd clearly see the following: Even if *every* team were as rich as the Yankees, an intelligently constructed league would still impose payroll caps and floors (at higher levels, of course).

Meanwhile, in the face of vast competitive imbalance and the owners' growing resolve, the Players Association and its knee-jerk supporters resort to red herrings, citing once pertinent arguments and numbers that now have little to do with the essence of the problem, as a way of dismissing it.

It's easy to see how this happens. Even the best organizations ossify over time, and the Players Association has been run by three people—Miller, Fehr, and Orza—for more than 30 years. Over that time, they have been unyielding, their ideological bent pushed to greater extremes by the bitter fights they endured. Their tactics have worked throughout that period because they were largely in the right, and the owners were disorganized, duplicitous, and collectively stupid. The owners' continued failure to present a convincing alternative meant the players never had to fully justify their position.

While the Players Association has been unchanging, the ranks of the owners, commissioners, and baseball management have shuffled numerous times. We've seen dozens and dozens of different owners and numerous commissioners, chief negotiators, and members of the management council. The owners have taken a circuitous path to the brink of what should be their logical position, almost like a drunk taking several wrong turns but somehow winding up at his front door. Even as individual owners still take actions that undermine their collective position, there is nonetheless a growing consensus among them that greater revenue sharing and other significant reforms are a must for the overall well-being of the sport.

What remains to be seen is if this group of owners can stick together, look beyond immediate self-interest and their disparate circumstances, and put forth a proposal that is actually good for them *and good for the players*. If that gets accomplished, and a fair deal is struck, Baseball might then be able to rationally consider issues like the wild card, realignment, postseason start times, and all the rest, and do it outside the present climate of economic crisis that often points them toward short-term revenue grabs rather than sound long-term baseball decisions.

Again, it is the owners who must take the initiative. The only way to test the players' willingness to be reasonable is to present them with a reasonable plan, and the sooner the better. By early in the 2001 season, the owners should first outline a comprehensive revenue-sharing plan as Bud Selig has promised and then present the players with a proposal whose main principles are bringing team payrolls closer together *and* improving the lot of rank-and-file players (the floor-to-ceiling salary cap proposal with a substantial increase in minimum salaries would accomplish both). Doing so in a timely fashion would give both sides plenty of time to negotiate before the threat of an imminent work stoppage is upon them.

Still, the owners are right to retain the threat of a lockout prior to the 2002 season, since without it they retain no real power of persuasion in the negotiations. (Used as a last resort, it need not be viewed as another disaster, but rather as a necessary step toward righting the ship.) But the public will support management's hard line stance *only* so long as it is in service of a worthy and visionary proposal. If owners break ranks among themselves, or use this crisis simply to try to reduce the players' overall compensation, they'll lose the public's support, lose the players, and send Baseball down a dead-end path. If they put forth a sound plan, I think they'll have the public's support, and I think they may earn something from the players they haven't had in a long time: their respect. Once that's been achieved, a solution is within reach.

I've never claimed to be an expert on the economic fine points or the nuances of collective bargaining, so I won't hazard a guess at whether the ultimate resolution will be closer to the plan you've read in this book or the solution outlined in the Blue Ribbon Panel's report or some more complex mechanism that hasn't been discussed yet. I am sure, however, that the ultimate answer rests upon the basic principles outlined in *Fair Ball*.

If the two sides put their narrow interests and long-harbored resentments aside long enough to honestly consider the best solutions for *the game* itself, then I'll be happy to have the owners, the Players Association, and their armies of lawyers and advisers work out the arcane particulars while I, along with millions of other baseball fans, stand back and applaud the sudden outbreak of good will and common sense.

Do I think that will actually happen?

This being baseball, hope springs eternal.

B.C.
January 2001

ACKNOWLEDGMENTS

I'd like to thank Michael MacCambridge for his editorial assistance with this book. My thanks also to all these fine people, who in one way or another, helped me to complete it: Sandy Alderson and Jeff White of Major League Baseball; Gene Orza of the Players Association; Charlie Conrad, Becky Cole, Bob Asahina, John Sterling, and Luke Dempsey at Broadway Books; Barry Frank and David Chalfant at IMG; Bill James and Dr. Richard G. Sheehan, who were consulted during the preparation of the text; Larry Schwartz and Pat Porter, who read the manuscript and provided numerous helpful suggestions; Marty Hendin, Kris Schwartz, Nick Acocella, and Ron Flatter, who provided research assistance; Sharon Maslow, for her transcription; Pam Davis and Kay Reller, in my office; Buzz Bissinger for his input in the early stages of the project; and Sloan Harris, Rick Pappas, Danica Frost, Arin Paske, and Suzy Gorman for their help throughout.

ABOUT THE AUTHOR

Bob Costas has won the Emmy Award as Outstanding Sports Broadcaster eight times and has been named National Sportscaster of the Year by his peers eight times. He has also received Emmy Awards for his writing, interviewing, and reporting. His coverage of major sports events includes the World Series, the Super Bowl, the NBA Finals, and the Olympics. In addition to his sports broadcasting, Costas hosted the Emmy Award-winning interview show *Later . . . with Bob Costas* on NBC. He will be hosting a new sports journalism program on HBO beginning in February 2001. A native New Yorker, Costas now lives in St. Louis.

All of Bob Costas's net proceeds from the sale of this book will go to B.A.T.—the Baseball Assistance Team, which provides financial assistance to those members of the baseball family in need. For more information contact: B.A.T., James J. Martin, director, 245 Park Avenue, 31st floor, New York, NY 10167. Phone: (212) 931-7822.

Printed in the United States
153144LV00002B/45/A